Reviews of
Searching for Tom Sawyer

"Tim Wright has hit this self-prescriptive disaster on the head. Fear-based parenting and the feminization of the church has led to over-protected and under-challenged boys who grow up to be spiritually passive men. Meanwhile a new generation of women cries out that men won't lead as they coddle and shelter their own boys. If we want strong men in our churches in the future, we need to make radical shifts now. Tim Wright has a sure fire cure for you, your family and your church."
>—Dr. Tim Kimmel, author of *Grace Based Parenting* and *Basic Training for a Few Good Men*

"More than 70% of the young men who are raised in church abandon it during their teens and twenties. Many will never return. Tim Wright examines the problem and offers real solutions to one of the greatest challenges facing the church today."
>—David Murrow, author of *Why Men Hate Going to Church*

*"No one who cares for boys, and equally no one who cares for kids and families should miss **Searching for Tom Sawyer**."*
>—Leonard Sweet, best-selling author of *Jesus: A Theography*, professor at Drew University and George Fox University, and chief contributor to sermons.com

"Pastor Tim has brilliantly demonstrated how the Church can capture the hearts and minds of our boys by giving us a plan for engaging and shaping them to become Strong Heroic Men!"
>—Dr Greggory Jantz, founder of *The Center*, and author of *Battles Men Face*

*"In **Searching For Tom Sawyer**, Pastor Tim Wright uses some of the latest insights from brain research and educational methodology to offer usable and practical guidance as well as encouragement for addressing how communities of faith might reverse the decades long trend of losing boys and men from our midst."*
>—Stephen S. Talmage, Bishop, *Grand Canyon Synod, Evangelical Lutheran Church in America*

"Tim's book brings awareness to an increasingly alarming crisis – the mass exodus of boys from our churches – and resulting leadership deficit of Godly men. He provides practical information and application for both parents and churches to address this issue. We must create a culture in our homes and churches that will lead boys into an exciting adventure with Christ and continued pursuit throughout adulthood."
>—Don Wilson, Sr. Pastor, *Christ's Church of the Valley*, Peoria, AZ

*"**Searching for Tom Sawyer** is a must read for congregations that long to reach and shape the hearts of boys and men for the Kingdom of God. Tim Wright's diagnosis of why most of our congregations struggle to connect with guys is eye opening and stunning. More importantly Tim provides practical strategies that can help congregations connect with and fire up the hearts of the Tom Sawyers all around us for God's mission. As the father of three boys I wish I'd had this book years ago. As the pastor of a congregation I'm glad I have it now.*
     —Pastor Jeff Marian, *Prince of Peace Lutheran Church*, Burnsville, MN

"Centuries ago the formal Church, despite evidence to the contrary, declared that the earth was the center of the universe, and took a stand that was inconsistent with truth as discovered in science. The church has been entrusted with the world's most important message – that of God's love for us in sending Christ. Despite the diminished involvement of men in the church, often the church clings to communicating this message in the same old way. Tim challenges the old wineskins of business as usual when he wisely integrates the science of manhood and a young man's development with the art of church leadership. His practical suggestions will encourage both boys and men to "follow Christ."
     —Roy Smith, creator and author of *Knights of the 21st Century*

"Tim Wright addresses a problem that has been largely hidden: the spiritual formation of boys. This book will deepen your understanding, challenge your status quo, and enlarge your circle. If there is a boy/man in your life, and you can't reach him for Christ, read this book. And then, let the adventure begin!"
     —Rev. Dottie Escobedo-Frank, pastor of *Crossroads United Methodist Church*, Phoenix, AZ and author of *Jesus Insurgency: The Church Revolution from the Edge* (with Rudy Rasmus)

"Why is men's ministry so hard? Why are there so few men in church? It's because we start losing them before the age of 9! Tim Wright has written a very important book that every parent and church leader should read. In **Searching for Tom Sawyer** *Tim Wright not only points out what the issues are with males—but he gives us parents and church leaders tools to deal with the issues, not from a legalistic "God's order" as some men's ministry is these days, but from a grace oriented theological perspective. The future, not only of what will become of men but of families and the church is at stake. This book gives us the tools, by God's grace, to help shape a bright future for each.*
     —Doug Haugen, Executive Director, *Lutheran Men in Mission*

"Tim Wright makes a compelling case for the way society has overcorrected on its past exclusion of women, now making it more difficult for boys to thrive in both academic and religious settings. **Searching for Tom Sawyer** *addresses the social, intellectual, and spiritual needs of boys—and provides reasoned and practical solutions to church and society's shortage of mature, moral adult men—all without denigrating women and girls in the process. Wright proves you can celebrate boys' need to be a hero without painting girls as damsels in distress."*
     —Jessica Miller Kelley, *MinistryMatters.com*

"Tim Wright has captured my imagination with his wit and wisdom. And he has opened my eyes to the incredible opportunity that lies before all of us to invest in the next generation. I can't think of a more important subject or more valuable insights for all who yearn for a better world!"

—Rev. Paul Sorensen, pastor of *Hope Church*, Phoenix, AZ

*"It is a confusing time in our culture and our churches on how to best move boys into manhood. Simply put we have lost our way. **Searching for Tom Sawyer** is a uniquely qualified book that will help guide parents and the church on how to forge our boys into the heroic men Jesus has called them to be. This book will change the way you look at boys and how we are called to raise them!"*

—Mike Ricker, founder of *Prodigal's Home,* a ministry to the homeless and at risk youth in Phoenix, AZ

*"**Searching for Tom Sawyer** is a powerful look at why boys and young men are opting out of church and how we as parents, congregations and leaders can reverse that trend. If we truly hope to raise up boys to become the strong and heroic men God created them to be, then we have no choice but to change how we motivate and empower them. In this book, Tim Wright offers up an easy-to-implement and engaging approach for families and churches to do just that!"*

—Kimberly Taylor, Owner & Consultant, *Taylor'd For Life*, business & life skills coaching

*"**Searching for Tom Sawyer** is a must read for all parents and church leaders. Tim Wright presents overwhelming evidence of a problem we should all be made aware of... the fact that the worldwide church today is losing its boys and young men at an increasingly alarming rate. More than that though... Tim offers his vast experience and insights, to provide a clear solution to this problem. Tim provides proven, practical applications on how we can best relate to our boys, and guide them to becoming the authentic life-giving men of God they were born to be."*

—Darren Lewis, Founder, facilitator, and fatherhood coach of *Fathering Adventures,* Queensland, Australia

*"**Searching for Tom Sawyer** has meat on the bone...a must-read for any faith leader who wants to help boys follow Jesus. This book will challenge you to not only think about boys and their faith, but will also give you the tools and direction to take action. If you have boys in your church, please read this book!"*

—Paul Nynas, Executive Pastor, *Hope Lutheran Church,* Fargo, ND

*"Some books are stuffy, outdated, and out of touch. Others are full of concepts but lack application. In **Searching for Tom Sawyer**, Tim Wright has given us a book containing content that is solid, relevant, timely, and practical. In its pages we discover real ways to impact the lives of boys and help them become all God has created them to be. I believe **Searching for Tom Sawyer** provides help and hope to all who influence the lives of boys.*

(Yes, that includes you and me!) I'm praying we'll accept the challenge Tim issues us: To understand and embrace our opportunity to help boys discover life lived God's way. That path will lead them to heroic manhood and a meaningful life!"
—Steve Swanson, Station Manager, *88.3 WAFJ*, Augusta, GA

"It's not a secret that children need supportive relationships with caring adults to thrive. But, as Tim Wright clearly advocates, parents are not always aware of how boys need men to love them 'malely,' to pass along to them their male vision, knowledge, energy, emotions, and spirituality. We see many boys raised by loving and extraordinary women, but with no male energy to pour into them. So the boys grow up with no idea of what it is to be a man and to how become one. The results…just look at the news or see what is happening to the inside of families' lives: times without a strong male vision are times without God, as he finds so much difficulty to be visible to humankind when fathers on Earth are not visible, either. If you believe in your heart you want to do something about this, or you hear the call of God to stand up for the cause of boys, girls, and families, you owe it to yourself to read this wonderful and inspirational book. It guides you on how it is to lead boys with a male vision of courage, nobility, and advocacy to family, and how to craft the kind of men God wants them to be."
—Gina Cuen, founding coordinator of a male tribe, Mexico

"As a pastor of 28 years – who happens to be a woman – within the Evangelical Lutheran Church in America, I applaud Pastor Wright's serious study of the relationship between boys and the church. Within this book are some of the keys, which will help move the church into the 21st century and help prepare boys to be heroes for God. Tim writes he 'still wants to save the world.' He may have done just that - or at least a small piece of it."
—Rev. Christine E. Erdmann, *Zion Evangelical Lutheran Church*, Gillespie, Illinois

*"Pastor Tim Wright presents an innovative perspective and practical ideas, which can be used in every congregation. He shows a path for how a congregation can reshape itself to become a more boy-friendly church. **Searching For Tom Sawyer** is a call for those who care about boys and care about the future of congregations."*
—Rev. Harri Palmu, Doctor of Theology, Psychotherapist, and Pastor, Finland

Tim is one of the best communicators I know. For the sake of the boys that God cares so deeply about, Tim has passionately championed their rescue from their endangerment of slipping away… away from our churches, and ultimately away from their place as Godly leaders of our families and society as a whole. Hard stuff to communicate. But Tim can. Tim does. With an understanding of what makes boys boys, Tim steps in with wisdom, facts, and experience to guide us in changing the story line of boys. Thank you Tim… for the sake of our boys.
—Terey Summers, comedienne, actress, motivational speaker, author of *If These Stretchmarks Could Talk*

Searching
for Tom Sawyer

How Parents and Congregations Can
Stop the Exodus of Boys from Church

TIM WRIGHT

With Foreword by Michael Gurian
Author of _The Wonder of Boys_ and _The Purpose of Boys_

WESTBOW
PRESS
A DIVISION OF THOMAS NELSON

WestBow Press books may be ordered through booksellers or by contacting:

WestBow Press
A Division of Thomas Nelson
1663 Liberty Drive
Bloomington, IN 47403
www.westbowpress.com
1-(866) 928-1240

ISBN: 978-1-4497-8620-5 (sc)
ISBN: 978-1-4497-8616-8 (e)

Library of Congress Control Number: 2013903465

Printed in the United States of America

WestBow Press rev. date: 03/11/13

The Adventures of Tom Sawyer by Mark Twain is public domain.

Scripture quotations not otherwise marked are taken from the NEW REVISED STANDARD VERSION. New Revised Standard Version Bible, copyright 1989, Division of Christian Education of the National Council of Churches of Christ in the United States of America. Used by permission. All rights reserved.

For Clover:
I pledge to be a "good man" in your life!
Grandpa

For Phoenix and Judah:
Follow me as I follow Jesus!
Grandpa

Table of Contents

Foreword

A great deal is at stake today for boys. At stake are boys' lives themselves, but also the lives of girls and women. As Tim Wright knows very well, our present era is one of gender interdependence. Everything going on with boys impacts girls, and everything men do or don't do impacts women. The systems of care and nurturing that we create for males and females need to fully understand and minister to both males and females.

I have worked with Tim for over seven years. In his vision and work I see a powerful realism about what our culture and its churches face every day: the loss of boys, and thus the harm to a world in which families, schools, churches, and communities try to flourish without half of their population engaged or present at the table. As a father of two daughters, I worry as Tim does that faith communities in sync with women's needs and not men's are set up to under serve both women and men, both boys and girls. So many people involved in faith communities do not realize how important gender interdependence is to the fruition of spiritual life. Tim is battling to increase that understanding.

In faith communities and churches, the loss of males is becoming especially epidemic, and that is the subject of this book. Churches used to include male necessity at their core mission; now, there is a softness to the male role, and males feel unnecessary. That softness came by historical necessity—for hundreds of years women struggled to have a voice in church and religion, and when they found that voice, it was seen immediately to be a voice that the modern church cannot thrive without. Women's increased role in church is sacrosanct.

But as that voice has emerged in religious life, the male voice has too much diminished, so that now our churches must ask: where has Tom Sawyer gone?

Where in the lifespan *of a church* is the boy who will push envelopes? We see that boy on sports fields, or becoming a man who climbs corporate ladders, but where is he in church? By early adolescence he has drifted away from God's house.

Where is the boy who will learn to love and serve and sacrifice *in his church?* Boys will learn much about love in their families, schools, and through the Internet, but they are growing into their teens without the spiritual anchor of church life to help shape them into whole men.

Where is the boy who will become the leader of men *in church?* While some men, such as Tim, hold positions of leadership, the next generation of leaders is increasingly women mentored by women. This would be a matter of wonder and pure grace if not for the fact that boys are drifting away from churches that do not include enough male role modeling, mentoring, and leadership to serve them.

Tim knows the questions to ask, and with almost thirty years of ministry behind him, he has answers. *Searching for Tom Sawyer* is a primer for church leaders and anyone associated with the structure and content of religious life. Tim's vision for males is male-positive and female-empowered. He is of a new generation of leaders who, I believe, have made peace with gender, and know how to advocate for one gender while also fully serving the other.

If this kind of gender balance is not incorporated soon in church life, spirituality will gradually become a realm of distrust for males. Boys will continue to feel that church cannot be entrusted with their souls—even with their growing, fidgety, visionary bodies and minds—and they will move away from God in ways that ultimately hurt themselves and others. Emptiness in the male soul is not what the world needs more of.

Thus, a great deal is at stake in this book, its ideas, and its practical strategies. I am hopeful that every church leader and friend of church will explore its pages with a sense of wonder—for Tom Sawyers are wonderers extraordinaire—and also a willingness to push the envelopes of church life toward a future that includes excitement and inspiration for even those somewhat wild boys a Sunday school teacher might be unsure of.

As Tim has said, "Every boy is a potential disciple of Jesus. It's our job as church leaders to show him we care enough about him to forge a congregation where he can feel inspired. If we do that, Jesus will find him."

--Michael Gurian, Author of *The Wonder of Boys*

Acknowledgements

Thanks...

To my family for all your love and support: Jan; Alycia, Corey, and Judah; Mike, Amber, Clover, and Phoenix

To Jeff and Diane: none of this happens without you!

To the Staff and Congregation of Community of Grace: it is an immense honor to join you in following Jesus on the bold, daring, reckless adventure of bringing grace to the world! I know of very few congregations as passionately committed to calling men, women, boys, and girls to follow Jesus than you.

To Michael Gurian: for your friendship, partnership, mentoring, and belief in me. It was a ministry game-changer when God brought the two of us together.

To all who wrote such kind endorsements for the book: Your words of support and encouragement affirmed my belief that we are on to something here.

To the many people at *WestBow Press* who worked with me to shape this into the best book possible.

To each of you reading this book: On behalf of boys, thanks for joining the revolution to change the story line of boys in the Twenty-first Century. May we have the courage to look them in the eyes and say: *Follow me as I follow Jesus!*

Preface

If you were to learn that the overwhelming majority of one of the sexes was in serious danger of becoming extinct from the church, what would you do as a parent? As a pastor? As a youth leader? As a Sunday school teacher?

Think about:

>	your son

>	your grandson

>	that boy in your Sunday school class

>	the boys in your youth group

>	the boys in your congregation

What if ...

>	The overwhelming majority of them left the Sunday school class/youth group/congregation and never came back?

>	The overwhelming majority of them entered manhood with no real vision for what it means to be a man?

Imagine:

>	A congregation with virtually *no* men!

>	A culture with fewer and fewer men living good, noble, honorable lives!

Wrap your mind around this:

> Seventy–ninety percent of all boys will leave the church in their early teens and twenties—and most will never come back!

Introduction:
Snips and Snails and Puppy Dog Tails

> There is no playbook for becoming an adult,
> no road map. Young men often feel they are
> making it up as they go along—in part, because
> they are.[1]
>
> "I am the Way, the Truth, and the Life!"
> —Jesus (John 14:6)

A young boy was walking down a dirt road headed home after church. He met a little girl walking in the opposite direction. "Hello!" said the boy.

"Hi!" replied the girl.

"Where are you headed?" asked the boy.

"I'm headed home from church," said the girl.

"So am I," replied the boy. "Which church do you go to?"

"I go to the Catholic church," said the girl. "Where do you go?"

"I go to the Lutheran church," answered the boy.

Because they were both about to turn down the same road, they decided to walk together. At one point, they came to a low spot in the road that was flooded from the rainstorm the night before. They couldn't figure out a way to get across it without getting wet.

"My mom will really give it to me if I get my Sunday dress wet," said the girl.

"My mom will do the same to me if I get my Sunday clothes wet," said the boy.

"I'll tell you what I'm going to do," said the girl. "I'm going to take off my clothes and hold them over my head as I cross through the water."

"Good idea. I'll do the same," said the boy.

They both took off all their clothes and walked through the water to the other side. As they stood in the sun waiting to dry off, the little boy looked the little girl over and said, "Wow! I didn't know there was such a big difference between Lutherans and Catholics!"

(Thanks to my friend Michael Gurian for this story.)

What Are Boys Made Of?

Parents and congregations today face one of the greatest challenges in Christian history: the mass exodus of boys and men from the church. The implications for parents and churches are profound, as we will discover. But first, it's important to take a quick—albeit overly simplistic—look back to see how we got to this point in the first place (which I'll tease out more in Chapter 1).

Back in the 1960s and 1970s, many parents and educators grew increasingly frustrated with the gap between boys and girls in school. Boys excelled in almost every area over girls. Because more boys attended college than girls, it gave them an advantage in the workplace over women. As a result, men flooded the job market while women stayed home, making women financially dependent on men.

The feminist movement addressed some of these issues by reminding the culture of the truth about girls and women: that they are equal to men. The feminist movement in many ways redefined womanhood, opening up the world to women, who dived in headfirst.

During that time, the government invested over one hundred million dollars to get girls caught up to boys in school. As a result, in the span of a generation, through the collective will of concerned parents, educators, men, women, and the government, we changed the storyline of girls and women in this culture. Girls and women have broken into almost every area of life once seen as the domain of men. (The 2012 Summer Olympics illustrated this point. For the first time, the US team included more female athletes than male. The entire 2012 Olympics were hailed as the year of women!) As the father of a focused, career-minded, want-to-change-the-world daughter who has a master's degree from London and a law degree from the University of Minnesota, I'm grateful for that change!

Our boys, however, ended up left in the dust. As we'll see in the next chapter, boys now lag far behind girls educationally, economically, and in the job market. On top of that, boys have no clear definition of what it means to be a man in this new world of equality.

One of the consequences, intended or unintended, of the feminist movement was the confusion between "equal" and "sameness," or the misunderstanding of differentness. Understandably, because girls and women were so far behind, it was important to stress that girls and women were not only *equal* to boys and men, but they could also *do* anything boys and men can do. Equal, however, came to mean "the same." Any differences between boys and girls, men and women, were downplayed, ignored, or denied.

In the 1980s and 1990s, this began to play itself out in the androgynization of boys and girls—i.e., trying to make them the same. Many tried to remove gender stereotypes by encouraging boys and girls to play with the same toys and read the same stories or by creating gender-neutral toys and stories.

The problem, however, wasn't so much the androgynization of boys and girls as it was the feminization of boys—and much of culture. (I use the word *feminization* throughout this book not as a negative term but as an expression of how something has been skewed to the sensibilities and brains of females.) What were seen as stereotypical male traits—aggression, hyperactivity, antsy-ness, fighting, etc.— were written off as bad. Many tried to remove gender stereotypes by trying to get boys to play with dolls rather than guns and by telling stories that were more relationship-oriented than action-oriented. Schools and churches increasingly "feminized" teaching, pivoting to the way a female's brain is wired to learn. The primary images of young men in magazines were of the soft, effeminate, chest-shaved model. Ironically, while trying to downplay stereotypes, many of these moves actually fed into them by trying to turn boys into girls.

While well-intentioned, these attempts at making boys and girls the same ended up robbing boys of who they are and of who they were created to be. And I would suggest that robbing boys of their boy-ness robs girls of their inherent girl-ness.

The "de-stereotyping" or feminizing of children continues today. In 2011, a story ran about a school in Sweden that refuses to use any gender-based language with the students. No more he or she, him or her. No longer referred to as "boys" or "girls," the children are introduced as "friends." Colors and toys are chosen so as not to promote stereotypes. A Canadian couple made the decision that they would not disclose the gender of their newborn baby. They didn't want anyone treating the child in a gender-biased or stereotyped manner.

For those of us called to raise, mentor, and/or disciple boys, whether as their mom, dad, grandma, grandpa, Sunday school teacher, youth leader, or pastor, understanding what makes a boy a boy is crucial. If we want to stop the exodus of boys from the church and its life-shaping call to follow Jesus, we need to recapture the spirit of what it means to be a boy. I'm not talking about stereotypes here (although just because it's a stereotype doesn't necessarily mean it isn't true or helpful). I'm talking about the essence of how a boy is created.

The Image of a Boy

As we think about reengaging our boys with the church through calling them to follow Jesus, it's good to go back to the very beginning ... a very good place to start. When you begin to read, you begin with ABC, and when you want to forge the spirit of a boy, you begin with Genesis 1:26–27.

> Then God said, "Let us make humankind in our image, according to our likeness; and let them have dominion over the fish of the sea, and over the birds of the air, and over the cattle, and over all the wild animals of the earth, and over every creeping thing that creeps upon the earth." So God created humankind in his image, in the image of God he created them; male and female he created them.

This theologically rich passage offers far more than this book can unpack. Two observations, however, will prove helpful throughout the rest of this adventure into boy-dom:

- *Male and female were created in the image of God*—Boys and girls are equally in the image of God. We need both male and female to get a full picture of the image of God.

- *God created humans male and female*—Although we are equal, we are different.

Those called to pour themselves into boys will want to hold both of these truths in equal tension. Emphasizing one over the other results in the following problems:

- By overemphasizing the differences, girls and women often end up feeling less than equal to men (or, as in today's society, boys and men feel inferior to girls and women).

- By overemphasizing equality (i.e., sameness) at the expense of differentness, we create the challenges boys are currently facing in an educational, work, and church world now skewed to the way girls and women are wired.

Boys are created in the image of God as boys. They are different from girls. Take off our clothes, and we see the physical differences. Take the clothes off of our brains, and brain research now confirms what most of us know intuitively and what the Bible says: We are equal but different.

If we want to raise heroic boys, if we want to call them to follow Jesus into compelling manhood, it's imperative that we understand how their Creator created them—how their brains work, how their brains process information, and how boys are wired to follow Jesus differently from girls. If we want to stop the hemorrhaging of boys leaving the church in droves, it's vital that we disciple them as boys— created as boys in the image of God.

The Quest for Boys—My Personal Adventure

I am a dad of two children: my firstborn, a daughter, and my second child, a son. I am also a grandfather of a granddaughter and two grandsons (so far). So I have some experience raising boys and girls. In raising my two children, I recognized their differences not only as a female and a male but also as two unique personalities. It wasn't until recently, however, that I began to truly understand the inherent differences between the sexes.

I've been a pastor since 1984. Like the overwhelming majority of church leaders, I used the discipleship tools available through Christian publishing companies. Most of them did not cater specifically to boys or to girls but offered mixed-gender programs. I didn't think twice about it. I did, however, at least subconsciously, recognize some of the differences in the ways boys and girls learn when I taught confirmation to seventh graders for the first time as a student pastor. Other than that, I never gave any thought to the differences between boys and girls and what that might mean for discipleship.

In 2005, I read a book by David Murrow entitled, *Why Men Hate Going to Church*. It was a no-holds-barred look at how feminized the church has become and how, as a result, men are staying away in en masse. David argues, correctly, that while men may still fill the pulpit, women overwhelmingly fill the pews. Subtly and not so subtly, we have skewed the gospel to the learning styles of women, leaving men behind.

David's book forced me to look at my ministry. And I saw a lot of things, obvious and not so obvious, that favored women over men. For example, the vision statement I had written for our congregation used lots of relationship and community language/images versus action language/images. So I rewrote our mission statement, making it action centered: "The mission of Community of Grace is to follow Jesus on the bold, daring, reckless adventure of bringing grace to the world." We reviewed the worship choruses we were using and nixed any and all that sounded like Top 40 love songs to Jesus. (I actually liked many of these songs because I understood what they were saying. But when I looked at the lyrics from the perspective of a man who perhaps had little or no Christian background, the words made me cringe: "Hold me close, let your arms surround me" … "Beauty that made my heart adore you" … "You're altogether lovely." Men don't generally speak—let alone sing—like this to other men. As David writes, imagine the mental gymnastics men have to go through while singing those songs to Jesus.) I rethought the way I talked about Jesus and moved away from a "Jesus wants a relationship with us" type message to "Jesus calls us to follow him" language. David's book stimulated my appetite to read and learn as much as I could about how to reach men.

David spoke at a worship service early on in our congregation's history. In eight minutes (because men aren't wired to sit for long sermons), he talked about how Sunday school tends to be stacked against boys. Sunday school is based on sitting still for long periods of time, which boys are not wired to do. It involves reading out loud, which boy brains don't do as well as girl brains at young ages. Boys have difficulty reading in front of the class and therefore find themselves embarrassed when the girls laugh at them. Girls excel in that environment, and boys know it. And before long, boys see Sunday school as girly. No wonder they end up leaving the church as soon as they can.

I immediately met with our Sunday school leaders. We separated the third through sixth grade boys from the girls of the same age, and I began writing the lessons for the boys, which included lots of activity and action-based learning. (See Appendix B.)

That prompted further learning for me. I began to read books about how boys and girls learn, which led me to Michael Gurian, the *New York Times* best-selling author of books like *The Wonder of Boys; A Fine Young Man; The Good Son; The Minds of Boys; The Purpose of Boys;* and *Boys and Girls Learn Differently*. Michael uses brain science research to enable us to better understand how boys and girls learn. His Gurian Institute has helped teachers and school districts around the country transform the way they teach boys and girls. I sent him an e-mail one day to see if he might be willing to do for our congregation what he had been doing for schools. To my surprise, he responded almost immediately. And that was the beginning of a friendship and partnership.

As we talked about how he might help our congregation, we turned to the subject of boys, Michael's passion. Michael comes from a Jewish background and knows from personal experience the power of rites of passage for boys, like the Jewish bar mitzvah. At that point, our congregation had no confirmation-type program. In over twenty-eight years of ministry, I had never found a confirmation program that I felt really discipled the students. Confirmation tends to pour theology, church history, and church polity into the students. But calling students to follow Jesus into noble manhood or dynamic womanhood and equipping them to do so didn't seem to exist in any of the programs I was aware of. So Michael and I decided to do something bold: To create a Christian rite of passage for junior high boys based on brain science research, rites of passage insights, mentoring (done primarily by the dads and using the program to disciple dads as well), and the call of Jesus to follow him into heroic manhood. Creating that kind of an experience for boys and their dads drove me even further into understanding how boys learn, how they hear the call of Jesus, and what it looks like to call boys to follow him.

Forging the Spirit of Boys

In this book, I want to introduce you to boys. I want to give you some insights into the challenges that many of them face in this new world. I want to provide some information on how God has wired the minds of boys—how it is they learn best and how they hear the call of Jesus. I want to offer you some practical ideas to get you started in your quest to stop the exodus of boys from your church while forging in them the call to heroic manhood through boy-brain discipleship. I want to suggest some resources that have been helpful for me in understanding boys. Ultimately, I hope to instill in you a vision for our boys—a vision that will call you, as it is doing for me, to learn all you can about boys. A vision that will move you to roll up your sleeves and do whatever it takes to love the boys in your life, enjoy them, and call them to follow Jesus into heroic manhood. I'm convinced that when we connect our boys to the bold, daring, reckless call of Jesus, it will re-connect them to the church as well.

Searching for Tom Sawyer

To help put a face to this vision, I want to use Tom Sawyer as our metaphor. In recent history, we have seen the release of several books about fictional boys, including Harry Potter and Percy Jackson. These stories follow in a long line of "heroic quest stories" that illustrate the quest a boy makes into manhood. But Harry and Percy, while capturing the essence of boys growing up, have magical powers and live in magical lands.

Tom, on the other hand, is the quintessential boy. He has no superhero or magical powers. Like every boy, he dreams of being a hero; he struggles with what it means to be a good boy; he gets into trouble; he can't sit still in school; he finds church boring; and yet, out of the blue, he does something so noble he leaves the adults in his life speechless. Tom represents the boys in our congregations. He also represents the boys leaving our congregations out of boredom, believing the church is only for girls. He puts a face to the call we have as parents and congregations to find our lost boys and call them to follow Jesus.

Every parent of a boy is raising Tom Sawyer in some manner. And every parent of a boy knows they need help in raising their son. That's why so many of them turn to the Boy Scouts or to sports programs and, sometimes, the church. Parents want to raise their boys into heroic manhood and know they need support in doing so.

Parents and congregations, partnering together, stand in a unique position in leading boys into manhood. We can call our boys to follow the One who, by his bold, reckless, active grace, is the path to manhood and the power for living a heroic life as a man.

Part 1

Searching for Tom Sawyer:
Boys in the Twenty-first Century

Picture:

> a boy in your congregation
>
> a boy in the Sunday school class you teach
>
> a boy in your confirmation class
>
> a boy in your youth group
>
> a boy you are coaching
>
> a neighborhood boy
>
> your son
>
> your grandson
>
> your nephew
>
> boys in general

Imagine:

Standing at the top of a summit with that boy. All of his life is in front of him.

> What are your hopes and dreams for him?
>
> What kind of life do you want him to have?
>
> What kind of a man do you want him to grow up to be?

1

Lost in the Twenty-first Century: A Story about Boys

"TOM!"

No answer.

"*TOM!*"

No answer.

"What's wrong with that boy, I wonder? You TOM!"

No answer.

The old lady pulled her spectacles down and looked over them about the room; then she put them up and looked under them. She seldom or never looked *through* them, for so small a thing as a boy; they were her state pair, the pride of her heart, and were built for "style," not service—she could have seen through a pair of stove lids just as well. She looked perplexed for a moment, and then said, not fiercely, but still loud enough for the furniture to hear:

"Well, I say, if I get hold of you, I'll—"

She did not finish, for by this time, she was bending down and punching under the bed with the broom, and so she needed breath to punctuate the punches with. She resurrected nothing but the cat.

"I never did see the beat of that boy!"

13

She went to the open door and stood in it and looked out among the tomato vines and "jimpson" weeds that constituted the garden. No Tom. So she lifted her voice at an angle calculated for distance and shouted,

"Y-o-u-u, *Tom!*"

There was a slight noise behind her, and she turned just in time to seize a small boy by the slack of his short jacket and arrest his flight.

"There! I might a-thought of that closet. What you been doing in there?"

"Nothing."

"Nothing! Look at your hands. And look at your mouth. What *is* that truck?"

"*I* don't know, aunt."

"Well, *I* know. It's jam—that's what it is. Forty times I've said if you didn't let that jam alone I'd skin you. Hand me that switch."

The switch hovered in the air—the peril was desperate—

"My! Look behind you, aunt!"

The old lady whirled round and snatched her skirts out of danger. The lad fled, on the instant, scrambled up the high board fence, and disappeared over it.

His aunt Polly stood surprised a moment and then broke into a gentle laugh.

"Hang the boy, can't I never learn anything? Ain't he played me tricks enough like that for me to be looking out for him by this time? But old fools is the biggest fools there is. Can't learn an old dog new tricks, as the saying is. But my goodness, he never plays them alike, two days, and how is a body to know what's coming? He 'pears to know just how long he can torment me before I get my dander up, and he knows if he can make out to put me off for a minute or make me laugh, it's all down again and I can't hit him a lick. I ain't doing my duty by that boy, and that's the Lord's truth, goodness knows. Spare the rod and spile the child as the Good Book says. I'm a-laying up sin and suffering for us both, *I* know.[1]

Tom Sawyer was born on a Monday at 5:35 a.m. after nineteen hours of labor. He weighed in at a healthy eight pounds. His mommy and daddy were understandably exhausted after the ordeal, especially Mommy. She had just given birth to a bowling ball, after all. Holding Tommy for the first time, however, erased all of that. The past nine months of pregnancy and the long hours in the delivery room faded as Mom and Dad looked at their son and dreamed about the life he would lead, the boy he would be, and the man he would become.

After getting some sleep, Dad headed to the local sports store. He bought Tommy his first football and football jersey. Mommy tried to get as much sleep as possible, having the responsibility for feeding her son, who, it turned out, had a very healthy appetite.

So began the writing of Tommy's story, a storyline shaped by Mommy and Daddy, grandparents, teachers, coaches, pastors, media, and a host of other influences in his life.

> *Steven Pinker, a professor of psychology at Harvard University, declares that there are sixty significant differences between males and females that have been discovered to date; some seem highly relevant to how we teach and raise boys.*[2]

Tommy's dad worked full time. His job involved travel about once a month for several days at a time. Mom, after taking six weeks off for maternity leave, headed back to her full-time job in marketing. Thankfully, Tommy's grandparents lived nearby to provide childcare during the workday.

The church was an important part of life for Tommy's mommy when she was growing up. Daddy came from a Christmas and Easter family. But both Mommy and Daddy agreed that the church should be a part of their lives ... if only they could find the time.

Tommy is a healthy boy. Developmentally, he's right on track. Everything works the way it's supposed to work from teething to crawling to taking his first steps. His dad and mom love him passionately. Like most parents, they dream of what's best for him and commit themselves to providing what he needs to succeed in life.

Tommy Heads to Preschool

When Tommy turns two, his parents, like many parents, begin thinking about preschool. Preschool is a fairly new phenomenon in our country. In the 1960s, about five hundred thousand kids attended preschool. (When I was a kid, the girl next door, about my age, *had* to go to *nursery* school. We all wondered what was wrong with her!) Today, preschool has become almost mandatory for preparing kids for elementary school. Over five million children are now enrolled in preschool—in part because of dual-income families; in part because of the belief that US students are falling behind the world educationally; and in large part because parents want to give their children every advantage possible to succeed in school and in life. To do this, we believe we need to get our kids started early. Years ago, preschool served primarily as a vehicle for kids to play and interact with other children. Today, it is seen as absolutely crucial for jump-starting a child's education.

Tommy's parents want him to succeed. Like many parents, they choose a highly structured, academically based preschool for their son. Their hope is that he will be reading by kindergarten. The reason: Kindergarten today looks much like first grade did back in 1978.

Tommy's parents' intentions are genuine and honorable. However, Tommy faces three major challenges with the type of preschool his parents chose for him:

1. *Tommy's boy brain is not wired to read at that age.* His brain is at least one year behind a girl's brain. The push to get him to read early—when his brain isn't ready for it—will set him up for frustration for the next several years. As his boy brain falls behind the reading expectations, he will learn at an early age that reading is not for him.

2. *Tommy's boy body is not wired to sit still for hours on end.* As we'll see later, his body is filled with testosterone—an action

hormone. His body needs to move! Highly structured, "sit, listen, and read" environments set him, his teachers, and his family up for disaster.

3. *Tommy's boy brain isn't developed enough to express feelings at that age.* In this area, he also lags behind girls. He can't articulate to his teacher why he's angry or sad or happy or even that he understands something.

The result: Boys are expelled from preschool at five times the rate of girls. They are four times as likely to be diagnosed with a learning disorder. And they are twice as likely to be held back.

By kindergarten, where children today are now expected to read, Tommy's five-year-old brain is developmentally that of a three-and-a-half year-old girl's brain. He's not yet ready to read or write. And it won't take him—or the others in his class—long to figure out who the dummies are: usually boys like Tommy. No wonder boys are 60 percent more likely to be held back in kindergarten than are girls.

Again, though well-intentioned, the lack of movement and the forced reading when his brain isn't ready for it may actually impede Tommy's school career from here on out.

Many Sunday school curriculums have bought into this emerging preschool model—one that favors the wiring of girls over boys. And many volunteers find themselves pulling out their hair each Sunday as they try to figure out how to keep the boys engaged and learning.

Tommy Moves into Elementary School

> Monday morning found Tom Sawyer miserable. Monday morning always found him so—because it began another week's slow suffering in school. He generally began that day with wishing he had had no intervening holiday, it made the going into captivity and fetters again so much more odious.[3]

17

Tommy is a bright boy. He's sharp. Intuitive. Funny. But he's falling behind in school. Sitting is the primary position of education, one that frustrates a testosterone-filled Tommy. Recess, essential for boys, seems almost a quaint idea from the last century. Thirty years ago, schools had two recesses a day. Tommy is lucky if he gets one a day. Recess is cut in favor of more learning (i.e., sitting) time. He has no outlet for working off his energy. So he does it in other ways. He fidgets. He squirms. He loses his attention quickly. He talks out of turn. It's not long before someone suggests to Tommy's parents that he might need Ritalin.

- For every 100 girls suspended from elementary and secondary school, 250 boys are suspended.

- For every 100 girls expelled, 355 boys are expelled.

- For every 100 girls diagnosed with a learning disorder, 276 boys are so diagnosed.

- For every 100 girls diagnosed with an emotional disturbance, 324 boys are diagnosed.

- Boys are three times more likely to be treated for ADHD

- Eighty-five percent of stimulant-addressing meds in the world are prescribed to boys in the United States.[4]

Tommy started falling behind in reading in preschool. Getting caught up with the girls is proving to be tough. Part of that has to do with the development of his brain versus the development of a girl's brain. Part of it has to do with the reading material itself. He doesn't like the reading assignments because so many of them seemingly skew to "girl" topics and the reading ability of girls.

Because of the fears generated since Columbine and similar events over the years, stories Tommy likes to read often have zero tolerance stamped on them. Tommy's boy brain tends to be drawn to action stories with fighting, death, and even some gore. In our understandable hypersensitivity-to-violence world, those kinds of stories have been discouraged. (The Bible is filled with great boy stories, but too often, we water them down, sanitize them, and soften them up.) For boys, however, these types of stories play an important role in their development. For boys, these stories are not about violence, but about sacrifice, fighting for friends, valor, courage, and honor. Obviously, such stories need some interpretation for younger boys. These kinds of stories, such as David and Goliath, Daniel in the lion's den, *The Lord of the Rings*, Jesus and the demoniac, Harry Potter, and others, speak to the hero boys dream of being and becoming. And such stories get boys reading!

Homework is based on reading and writing skills. As Tommy falls more and more behind, his frustration grows. He sees few men reading. The stuff he's assigned to read is too girly or he can't read it, so he convinces himself that reading is for girls and that school in general is for girls. This is reinforced by the fact that most of his teachers are female. In the long term, his career choices shrink as reading and writing have become essential for employment today.

> *Seventy percent of all Ds and*
> *Fs are given to boys!*

In fourth grade, the reading curriculum changes. Students are expected to move from learning to read to reading to learn. This creates what many educators refer to as a "fourth grade slump" made up of those, mostly boys, who still can't sound out words.

This leads to the "eighth grade cliff" where boys like Tom (he dropped Tommy in third grade) fall so far behind in reading, and therefore in grades, that he wants to give up. Which leads to the "ninth grade bulge." Ninth grade tends to have more students than eighth or tenth grade because of those, mostly boys, who were held back in ninth grade.

> *Over the last twenty years, the reading skills of seventeen-year-old boys have steadily declined!*

Tom and College

> *Policymakers in the United States calculate that if 5 percent more boys completed high school and matriculated to college, the nation would save $8 billion a year in welfare and criminal justice costs.*[5]

Boys like Tom are increasingly no-shows in college. Many colleges across the United States have reached a tipping point where at least 60 percent of the enrollees are women. Girls are better prepared for college than are boys because:

- More girls than boys take college prep classes in high school.

- Girls get better grades than boys and graduate from high school with higher GPAs.

- More girls than boys take the SAT.

- More girls than boys get involved in extracurricular activities.

Some colleges are quietly using a new form of affirmative action: passing over qualified women to accept less qualified young men. The young men who do enroll in college are more likely to drop out than girls. Tom is less likely to get a college degree than his own dad. And in today's world, a college degree is vital—it's the equivalent of a high school diploma from thirty years ago.

The Changing Life-Script of Men

On top of the educational challenges boys like Tom face, add in the changing, uncertain life-script of men. Feminism helped rewrite the life-script of women (although women seem to be more conflicted than ever over what it means to be a woman). What it didn't do, however, was help men and women rethink what it means to be a man in this new world.

At the risk over oversimplifying, the life-script of men used to consist of three primary responsibilities:

- creating a family

- providing for the family through work

- mentoring the children, especially boys

Women no longer need men to create children. They can adopt or they can use a local sperm bank. A man is no longer essential in creating a family. Women no longer need men to provide for them financially. Today, young adult women are making more money than young adult men.

While boys still desperately need men to lead them into manhood, most first world cultures have all but lost any rites of passage experiences for boys. Forty percent or more of boys will spend at least a part of their growing up years without a dad. In an inner city area where our congregation has a mission, that number is 70 percent! Our boys don't have men to look them in the eye and say, "This is what a man looks like."

Our boys are lost as to what it means to be a man because so many men are lost as to what it means to be a man. Where there is no clear,

21

compelling vision for manhood, boys will make it up as they go, more often than not falling into stereotypes: the cardboard macho man or the more popular man-vision today, the boy in a man's body—i.e., permanent adolescence.

Tom Quits Church

> Now the minister prayed. A good, generous prayer it was, and went into details ... (Tom) did not enjoy the prayer, he only endured it, if he even did that much. He was restive all through it; he kept tally of the details of the prayer, unconsciously—for he was not listening, but he knew the ground of the old, and the clergyman's regular route over it—and when a little trifle of new matter was interlarded, his ear detected it and his whole nature resented it; he considered additions unfair, and scoundrelly ... The minister gave out his text and droned along monotonously through an argument that was so prosy that many a head by and by began to nod ... Tom counted the pages of the sermon; after church, he always knew how many pages there had been, but he seldom knew anything else about the discourse ... (H)e lapsed into suffering again, as the dry argument was resumed.[6]

Many of the challenges Tom faces in the education system he also faces in church. Think about the typical Sunday school class for a moment (or worship service, for that matter). Just like school, Tom sits for up to an hour, trying to read a story or listen to a teacher talk about a story. The girls read better than he does, which shames him. He doesn't comprehend the concepts as quickly as the girls, which shames him even more. He may color a picture, but generally speaking, he's not moving. The learning environment is not conducive to his boy brain. Typically, the "discipline challenges" come from the boys. If he doesn't like school, he's not going to like Sunday school.

Just as he comes to believe that school is girly, he thinks the same about church. Most of the teaching methods serve girls better. Most of those teaching him are women. He's constantly being told to simmer down, to be quiet, to stop running, to stop talking. Church makes him feel worse about himself. If he's attending a church that uses "contemporary music," he's singing mushy love songs to Jesus, who seems more like a girl's boyfriend than a man to follow. He rarely sees men reading the Bible, with the exception perhaps of the pastor. He has few men to mentor him. His dad rarely if ever goes to church, in spite of the commitment he made to his wife when Tom was born. Nothing in his church speaks to him as a man in the making. The only rite of passage he'll attend, against his will, is a confirmation program, based on reading and theological abstracts. Tom senses something deep inside that wants to connect with his Creator. But the connections the church offers him don't speak to his boy brain.

Boys like Tom are lost in the twenty-first century. The Christian church, too, is lost when it comes to captivating boys like Tom.

Questions

- Where will that kind of a storyline lead boys like Tom?

- With the current educational storyline, where will these boys get jobs once they become men?

    o Eighty percent of the fastest growing careers will require a post-secondary education

    o The overwhelming majority of the fastest growing careers cater to the abilities and wiring of women

- What kinds of jobs will these boys get?

- o Almost 1 in 4 boys with college-educated parents can't read a newspaper with understanding

- How can Tom possibly survive in an information age dependent on reading, writing, and comprehension in light of the current education storyline for boys?

- What kind of woman will want to marry someone like Tom? A young man with no college education, no skills for the new economy, and no sense of what it means to be a man?

- How will society absorb these men?

- What is the responsibility of the Christian church to advocate for boys and take the lead in changing their storyline?

- How will the Christian church stop the flow of boys and men out of the church?

- What will the church look like if it keeps hemorrhaging boys and men?

- How will the Christian church effectively and meaningfully call boys like Tom to follow Jesus into compelling manhood?

- How does the gospel, how does Jesus, change the storyline of boys?

Why are the bad kids always boys?

—Second grade girl[1]

2

Why Do Boys Do That?

Now every year his parents went to Jerusalem for the festival of the Passover. And when he was twelve years old, they went up as usual for the festival. When the festival was ended and they started to return, the boy Jesus stayed behind in Jerusalem, but his parents did not know it. Assuming that he was in the group of travelers, they went a day's journey. Then they started to look for him among their relatives and friends. When they did not find him, they returned to Jerusalem to search for him. After three days, they found him in the temple, sitting among the teachers, listening to them, and asking them questions. And all who heard him were amazed at his understanding and his answers. When his parents saw him, they were astonished; and his mother said to him, *"Child, why have you treated us like this? Look, your father and I have been searching for you in great anxiety."* (Luke 2:41–48, emphasis added)

A friend sent me an e-mail with the header, "Why Boys Need Parents." The e-mail consisted of several pictures of boys about to do something really stupid and reckless. Picture in your mind:

- A young boy standing on a skateboard at the top of a steep hill in San Francisco about six blocks long, ending at a pier jutting into the ocean

- A young boy sticking a knife into an electrical outlet

- A boy with a huge frog stuck partially in his mouth

- A boy standing on the roof of his house, dumping a bucket of water on his unsuspecting grandpa sitting below

- A boy with feminine pads stuck all over his naked body and wrapped conveniently around his penis

Why do boys do that?

- On the weekend before Halloween, we told the kids they could wear their costumes to church. During the Saturday evening service, I invited the kids up front to introduce themselves and who they were dressed up to be. One of the small boys was dressed up as the Incredible Hulk. He was quite shy and hesitant to say his name. Just as I was about to send the kids back to their parents, a small Spider-Man came running up. I asked him if he thought his Spidey web was strong enough to hold the Hulk. He immediately jumped in front of the kids and pretended to spray his Spidey web at the Hulk. The Hulk instantly responded by putting on his mask. He then jumped off the small platform and began duking it out with Spider-Man. Without warning, they both spontaneously ran out of the worship center, continuing their epic battle. It was nothing short of awesome!

Why do boys do that?

The Action Hormone

In a word: *testosterone.* Boys are made up of more than testosterone just as girls are made up of more than estrogen. But for boys, testosterone is a defining hormone. It's essentially what makes a boy a boy in the womb. Testosterone shapes a boy and the way he behaves. It's an energy hormone. Testosterone serves as a powerful metaphor for understanding boys and how we can call them into noble manhood.

Michael Gurian, in his book *The Wonder of Boys,* outlines some of the boy-shaping qualities of testosterone[2]:

- *Testosterone is the defining agent of whether a fetus will be male or female.* We all start out as females in the womb. Testosterone makes the male male.

- *Testosterone is an aggression and physical risk-taking hormone.* Aggression, action, and risk-taking are hardwired into boys. As Michael notes, aggression does not equal violence. Violence is taught. Aggression is hardwired and can be forged into a powerful, positive tool in the life of boys. Testosterone is the God-given energy that enables boys to save the world.

- *Testosterone expresses itself in the need to move and do things.* Ever notice how hard it is for boys to sit still? They squirm. They fidget. They tap things. They distract easily. When you understand how testosterone works, you understand why boys move all the time. And you understand why boys are best discipled and taught through action, doing, and movement. "Follow me," Jesus says. "Move with me … act with me … do what I do". You also understand why boys bond with others better through doing than through talking. Jesus almost always uses action language in bonding with his disciples.

- Because of testosterone, boys on average will:

    o turn toys into guns and swords more often than girls

    o hit more

    o try to "one up" more

- o   tend to be less in tune to the pain of others

- o   generally be more competitive

- o   seek rough-and-tumble play

- *Testosterone-driven boys tend to seek independence earlier than girls.* But they still need to feel safe in Dad and Mom's love.

- *As he moves into puberty, he will have five to seven surges of this action-oriented hormone each day.* And we want him to sit still and listen to a Sunday school lesson for an hour!? No wonder he's bouncing off the walls!

- *He will be quicker to act physically to external stimulation.*

- *He will tend to move to problem solving even in the face of emotionally complex experiences.* Wives and girlfriends recognize this one. Almost always, when verbalizing a challenge they are dealing with, their husband or boyfriend immediately steps in to try to fix it.

- *He will often look for activities that will help him release the buildup of testosterone, like playing sports or focusing energy on a specific task.* A boy-driven approach to discipleship will find ways to utilize this buildup of energy to lead the boy into following Jesus.

The Bias against Testosterone

One afternoon, I was at my granddaughter's house. She was watching a cartoon designed for young preschool children. In each show, the cartoon teaches a lesson about getting along with others or about diversity. The main character is a girl who has three male animal friends.

In this particular episode, one of the boys was acting like a boy. He was a bit rambunctious. He wanted to move, play, and make noise. But the other two boys were having nothing to do with it. Each time he splashed them or ran a circle around them, they would whine and say, "He's being rough!"

The girl character taught them a new song. "Don't be rough … be gentle." Each time the boy got rough (which he never really was, just a boy moving and playing), the other boys would whine, berate the "rough" boy, and sing, "Don't be rough … be gentle."

The longer I watched, the more my testosterone began to boil. On so many levels, this cartoon was teaching the wrong lesson. Rather than helping that boy harness his energy in appropriate ways, the lesson essentially said that boy behavior is always wrong. Never be rough. Always be gentle. Never once were the whining boys encouraged to stop their whining. Instead, their whining led to the rough boy being told to stop acting like a boy!

That same bias against testosterone is practiced over and over again in subtle and not-so-subtle ways. Every time boys are made to sit quietly for extended periods of time and then reprimanded for moving, they are being told that boy behavior is bad. After all, who is usually rewarded for the "good" behavior of sitting still and listening? Girls.

Education and discipleship that favors sitting, listening, talking, relating, and emoting over action subtly tells boys that building things and moving means there is something wrong with them.

Jesus understood the power of testosterone to get things done. He was constantly on the move. He constantly taught his disciples on the fly. He would *do* something (heal the sick, fight a storm, cast out a demon, or feed the hungry). Then he would ask the disciples to *do* it too. Yes, there were times of teaching. And yes, testosterone-charged boys *can* sit and listen. But the primary way to engage them is through action-oriented learning—the kind Jesus used. (And remember, Jesus often taught his disciples as they were out walking.)

The call to discipleship for boys is the call to harness the power of testosterone for the cause of Jesus. To forge and shape that testosterone-driven energy for good, noble, grace-based purposes. To invite boys to utilize their power to join Jesus in building the kingdom of God:

a kingdom of grace, compassion, forgiveness, justice, and love. That happens when we call boys to *follow* Jesus; when we call them to an action-oriented form of discipleship.

Other Things You Want to Know about Boys

As testosterone begins to blitz the male fetus, it impacts the development of the boy's brain. A boy brain is different from a girl brain. It processes information and emotions differently. It learns differently. Therefore, it follows that it will be "discipled" differently as well.

A boy brain:

- Tends to favor the visual over the verbal

A girl's brain has better connectivity between both halves of the brain, allowing her, among other things, to process words better than does a boy. Another way of saying it is that both sides of her brain talk to each other better than does a boy's brain. Her "brain talk" makes reading easier for her. That's not to say that boys can't and shouldn't read. It simply means that it can be more challenging for boys. It also means that pictures, metaphors, and stories speak to boys better than merely verbal lectures.

Think about the typical religious education. It's based on sitting still, listening to someone talk, and focusing on reading a sacred text. This favors a girl's brain. Add into that mix pictures, videos, hands-on metaphors, and then you begin to capture the boy as well. There are three reasons why the market for video games is overwhelmingly boys—action, movement, and pictures. There's a reason why Jesus spoke so often in stories and used word pictures—he was speaking primarily to men. When I was a boy, flannel boards were the rage. I can still remember the stories of Samson and David and other biblical heroes "moving about" on the flannel board. What is today's flannel board for boys?

- Tends to process emotions slowly

Because a girl brain has better connectivity between both sides of the brain, a girl processes events and emotions together. She can almost instantly tell you what she's feeling the moment you ask her. She can remember what she felt when a certain event happened because the event and the emotion are remembered together. Boys tend not to process event and emotion, so they have a much harder time (as do men) talking about how they feel. Asking how a character in a story might have felt is daunting for a boy who has a hard enough time articulating his own feelings. That's not to say that boys don't feel. They feel deeply. But they often can't find the words to connect their thoughts and feelings.

- Tends to internalize

Girls generally process more words than boys, meaning in an average day they will speak and/or read more words than will boys. Girls tend to do their thinking out loud—talking through their issues to a resolution. Boys tend to internalize their thinking, in part because they don't want to appear stupid. They think through an issue internally first and then give the answer. That can make for a challenging give-and-take in the classroom. The leader asks a question and often gets one of the following responses from boys:

a blank stare

an "I don't know"

a monosyllabic answer

Again, this happens in part because boys need time to internalize their thinking before they answer.

- Tends not to pick up on nuance

Girls hear better than do boys. They have a stronger sense of smell than do boys. Their sense of touch is more sensitive. They are more attuned to the ambiance around them than boys, taking in the verbal and visual cues better. One simple way to engage boys better is to speak a bit louder. Not in a way that frightens them, but in a way that helps them hear. Many boys are disengaged simply because they can't hear well! Since they aren't as attuned to the nuance of the lesson or the facial expressions of the leader, activity keeps them plugged in: movement, games, competition, writing down their thoughts, etc.

A Few Final Things You Want to Know about Boys

I love words. My life's work centers in large part around words. I write words. I speak words. I read words. I enjoy listening to a good, articulate speaker (although I find myself constantly moving and shifting and fidgeting).

I don't like building things. I got a D in seventh grade shop class. I turned in my metal napkin holder in several pieces. I had no patience or desire to do anything in shop class.

We have a wall full of tools in our garage. We have a sanding machine and a jigsaw. They all belong to my wife. I don't fix things. Usually, if I put something together, I mess it up the first time and then the second and in the process turn the room blue with language not appropriate for a good Christian man!

I'm not into cars. I don't get car shows. I don't understand spending hours in the garage on a Saturday morning, fixing a car. God created car repair garages for a reason—so I don't have to change my oil!

I was a band geek—although at our school, the concert band was well respected. I played trumpet. I sang in choirs and bands. I played bass guitar.

I love sports. But I wasn't necessarily great at team sports. I was the first person in the history of T-ball to actually strike out. I sat on the bench most of the year in tenth grade B-squad basketball. But I ran three marathons and seven half marathons in my forties and early fifties, and today, I enjoy riding my road bike. I'm a big fan of the Arizona Cardinals (I went to their Super Bowl!), the Adelaide Crows, and the Sydney Swans (Australian Rules Football). I enjoy competition. I hate losing. But I have no knack whatsoever for video games.

Boys come in different shapes and sizes. While generally speaking boys have a tougher time with words than do girls, that's not true for all boys. While boys tend to like working on things and building things, that's not true for all boys. While some boys like athletics, others like music. Many boys will find an academic-based preschool difficult to navigate while others will thrive in that environment. Some boys can talk up a storm in Sunday school, and other boys will have a hard time articulating their thoughts. Some wear their emotions on their sleeve while others fight hard to keep their emotions inside.

But for all the differences, testosterone plays the great leveler. Verbal or not, boys have an energy that yearns to be harnessed for good. Athletic or not, boys want to move as they learn. They learn best when learning comes visually and metaphorically.

Ultimately, deep down inside each boy is the God-created desire to matter, to make a difference in the world, to be a good boy who grows up to be an honorable man. Inside each boy is the yearning for a vision he can grow into—a vision Jesus calls him into with two powerful words: *Follow me!*

Part 2

Forging the Spirit of Boys:
Changing the Storyline of Boys

3

A Motivating Affirmation for Life

In tenth grade, I played on the B-squad basketball team. I use the word *played* generously, as most of the time I sat on the bench. I really wasn't that good—but I enjoyed playing, and I knew my role on the team: to provide someone to play "against" during practice and to give the starter a minute or two to breathe during the game.

The coach had a rule that year: Miss a game for any reason, and you were automatically benched the entire next game. I had to miss a game that season to attend the retirement party of my grandpa, who was a Lutheran pastor and a primary shaper in my life. I was not going to miss his big party. And since I sat on the bench anyway, it wasn't a big deal for me to miss a game. The coach understood my reason for skipping the game but told me I would be benched the following game.

The team lost that night and lost badly. And the coach was furious. So he decided to mix things up. When I came to practice the next day, I found that instead of being benched, I was now starting the next game! For several days, I practiced as the new starter. The guy I replaced wasn't happy about it and harassed me throughout the practices, telling me the coach had no confidence in me.

Then it was game night. My pre-game meal: A coke and French fries from Kentucky Fried Chicken. Big mistake. Coke and fries rumbling around a nervous stomach!

Right before the tip off, our cheerleaders hit the floor to introduce the team. For the first time, one of those cute cheerleaders said, "Tim, Tim, he's our man, if he can't do it, no one can!" In spite of the fries churning in my gut, I was psyched. And I played the game of my life.

We were playing for first place against a team that beat us earlier in the season. I defended well. I made a couple of baskets (I was not a prolific scorer) and single-handedly sent the game into overtime. We were behind by two points with only seconds left. As I dribbled the ball up court, I was fouled. It was a one-on-one free throw. If I made the first shot, I would get a second one. By now, the gym was full, as people had come to see the A-squad play for first place and were cheering for us like we were the A-squad. We'd never experienced that before. *And I had the chance to tie the game.*

I dribbled the ball a few times. I looked at the basket and took the shot ... and just as I planned (tongue in cheek), the ball hit the left side of the rim, bounced into the hands of our best shooter, who made the basket and sent the game into overtime ... which we won!

After the game, I was in the locker room, getting ready to shower. It was a whole new experience for me, as I'd never broken a sweat in a game before. Suddenly, the coach walked out of his office and over to me. He didn't speak to anyone else. He shook my hand, said, "Great game!" and then headed back into his office.

To this day, I remember everything about that affirmation. While it didn't make me a better player (I ended up back on the bench in the middle of the next game after stinking up the joint), it did forge in me a new sense of confidence.

Years later, I was attending the Lutheran Bible Institute in Seattle, Washington, part of my college education experience. One day during chapel, I got up and made a one-minute announcement. Afterward, a teacher whom I deeply admired came up to me and said, "You have a special gift for preaching." From that moment on, he was for years a source of affirmation for me as a preacher in the making.

The Power of Affirmations

Affirmations forge power, hope, joy, tenacity, and faith in a boy. Affirmations say, "This is who you are. This is who you can be. This is who I see you to be." When that affirmation comes from a respected male in his life, that passing of male energy inspires greatness in a boy. When that affirmation comes from his father, it sets him on a course for heroic manhood.

Just before Jesus launched his three-year quest to the cross, he received what every boy needs to be a man: the blessing of his Father. As Jesus came up out of the waters of baptism, his Father affirmed him with these words, "You are my beloved Son. I am fully pleased with you." (Mark 1:11, *author's paraphrase*)

Imagine for a moment the identity issues Jesus must have wrestled with while growing up. Imagine, for example, the rumors about his birth father. One persistent rumor was that he was the bastard son of a Roman soldier. His mom and dad, on the other hand, told him he was the Son of God. Think about what that would do to your psyche. Jesus, being fully human, must have wrestled with his identity because so many of us do. As he got older, he had a sense he was different from the other kids, that there was a compelling call on his life. But how could he know for sure?

Then his Father stepped in and blessed him. He affirmed Jesus with the words every boy yearns to hear from his dad, "I love you, and I am proud of you."

Immediately, that affirmation was tested for forty days. Again and again, Satan said to Jesus, "So you think you're the Son of God? Let's try it out and see if it's true." Armed with a memorable affirmation from his Father, Jesus was able to resist the temptation. He knew who he was because his Father told him who he was. His dad's affirmation gave him the power to live out his calling.

Jesus received those words of affirmation again on the Mount of Transfiguration just before he went to the cross. Once again, following that blessing, his identity was called into question. First in Gethsemane, you can hear the anguish in Jesus' soul. "Really, Dad, this is what it means to be your son?" But his Father's blessing enabled him to say, "Father, not my will, but yours be done." (Luke 22:42, *author's paraphrase*)

On the cross, Jesus entered into God-forsakenness and cried out, "My God, My God, why have you forsaken me?" (Mark 15:34) Or again, "Really, Dad, this is what it looks like to be your son?" Could it be that in that moment of seeming abandonment the words he heard in baptism and on the mountain came back to him? "You are my beloved son. I am fully pleased with you." For with his waning breath, he was able to say, "Father, into your hands I commend my spirit." (Luke 23:46) If Jesus needed to hear those words, imagine how much more our boys need to hear them and hear them often.

The Hole in a Man's Soul

> *The last thing we want is for men to carry empty souls in their big bodies.*[1]

If you dig deep enough into the soul of a man who for some reason seems a bit lost in life, or maybe real lost, you'll usually find a man who never received affirmation from his father. In groups, I often ask men, by a show of hands, how many *never* received a blessing from Dad. More often than not, the overwhelming majority of men raise their hands. In a session on manhood I was leading, a group of four high school boys talked about their dads and the lack of Dad's blessing in their lives. One boy said, "The best thing my dad did for me was leave!" Do you hear the pain?

My dad was the second child of four kids. His dad, an alcoholic, left the family when the kids were very young. Essentially, my dad grew up in poverty as a result. Dad understandably carried a deep anger toward his father. At one point, when his dad tried to pop back into their lives as he often did, only to leave again, they came to blows, as my dad demanded that his father stay away.

Thankfully, my dad didn't pass that father wound onto us. But he lived with that wound all of his life. It wasn't until I was an adult myself that I began to understand how that father wound shaped my dad's life. My dad was always fighting someone or something. Turns out, in the end, he was fighting his dad. It's part of what made my dad such a success. He didn't back down from a fight. But it's also part of what led to many of my dad's failures. He was fighting his dad, and it blinded him at times.

Months before my dad died, he attended a class on manhood I

was teaching. Near the end of the course, I happened to sit in on his small group as the men talked about heroes in their lives. My dad stunned me when he told the group that his biggest hero was his dad. He said he admired his dad because he never backed down from a fight. I thought to myself, *Are you kidding me? This man abandoned Grandma and you for a younger woman. He was an alcoholic. You grew up in poverty because of that man. You've carried a lifelong wound from that man!*

But I've seen this happen now many times with men carrying a father wound. Dad has wounded them deeply, but the little boy in them still needs Dad to be a hero. My dad, though I'm not sure he knew it, was really expressing the universal need of all boys: the need for his father's approval.

Without Dad's blessing, a boy struggles to be whole. With Dad's blessing, a boy's spirit is forged with noble, good, life-affirming power.

> *(The male's) love of sports may also be about connecting with one person in particular—the one person who has the power to validate your manhood or dissolve it in an instant: Dad.*[2]

Stepping into the Hole

As pastors, church leaders, youth leaders, and Sunday school teachers, we can play an important role in forging the spirit of boys with motivating affirmations. To begin with, we can provide opportunities where dads can learn to affirm their sons (and daughters).

We "stole" an idea from another church a couple of years ago. We held a Man-Cave, All-You-Can-Eat BBQ. I had the dads bring their sons. Grandpas, dads, and sons came out for some games and great food. Then I had each of the men bring their boys up front, one dad and son at a time, and had them introduce their sons, tell us one thing about them they were proud of, and then publically say to their sons, "I love you." For some dads, it was the first time they had

41

ever given their son a blessing. For some older men, whose dads were there with them, it was the first time they received a blessing from their father. I make it a priority to regularly remind dads to bless and affirm their sons—to say to them, "I love you. I'm proud of you," and to affirm their gifts and talents.

We can also be the voice of blessing for boys who don't have a dad or for boys whose dads aren't in a place where they can give a blessing. During that Man-Cave BBQ, I asked one of my leaders to come forward. He, like my dad, lives with a huge father wound. So as his spiritual father and friend, I publically affirmed him, telling the other men about how proud I was of him and that I loved him.

A sincere "Teddy, I really like you" or "Juan, I am so impressed by how you do that" can forge power in a boy. Catching a boy in the act of acting nobly and commenting on it lifts his confidence and inspires him to continue to pursue an honorable manhood.

Ultimately, we can be the voice of God for our boys, to say to them in a variety of ways and in a variety of circumstances, "You are God's son. He is proud of you, and he loves you." As a part of our Rite of Passage Celebration (see Chapter 5), I publically speak those words to each boy as he stands in front of the congregation. How might your congregation find ways to bless your boys with God's words of affirmation?

Affirming a boy with God's grace shapes a boy into a heroic man. It helps him hear the call of Jesus on his life. Once blessed, however, he needs a compelling vision to live into.

4

A Compelling Vision for Life

Just here the blast of a toy tin trumpet came faintly down the green aisles of the forest. Tom flung off his jacket and trousers, turned a suspender into a belt, raked away some brush behind a rotten log, disclosing a rude bow and arrow, a lath sword and a tin trumpet, and in a moment had seized these things and bounded away, barelegged, with fluttering shirt. He presently halted under a great elm, blew an answering blast, and then began to tiptoe and look warily out, this way and that. He said cautiously—to an imaginary company:

"Hold, my merry men! Keep hid till I blow."

Now appeared Joe Harper, as airily clad and elaborately armed as Tom. Tom called:

"Hold! Who comes here into Sherwood Forest without my pass?"

"Guy of Guisborne wants no man's pass. Who are thou that—that—"

"Dares to hold such language," said Tom, prompting—for they talked "by the book," from memory.

"Who are thou that dares to hold such language?"

"I, indeed! I am Robin Hood, as they caitiff carcase soon shall know."[1]

When I was a boy, I wanted to be Batman. Not the Christian Bale Batman. Or the handsome George Clooney Batman. Or the Val Kilmer Batman. Or the Michael Keaton Batman. I wanted to be the *real* Batman. The 1960s, Adam West Batman. I wanted the adventure of having a secret identity; of fighting bad guys; of driving that cool Batmobile and using all of those cool Bat-toys. My mom made me a Batman cowl out of a sheet, and I ran around the yard, pretending to be Batman. I wanted to be a hero. Still do. I still want to save the world.

Boys begin life dreaming of being a hero. We want to be superheroes. We want to be firefighters. We want to be star athletes. We want to be soldiers. We want to fly faster than a speeding bullet and leap tall buildings in a single bound. No boy dreams of being a dud, loser, slacker, thug, or passive, inept couch potato. Every boy hears the call of his Creator for heroic living. (See Appendix A, "Can't Girls be Heroes Too?")

Sadly, however, often in early adolescence, many boys lose their way. The journey into manhood begins to weigh on them as they try to navigate their changing bodies, their out-of-control emotions, the culture of boy cruelty, girls, and, for many, an increasingly tough slog through school. For many boys, the vision of being a heroic man gets beaten down. But it never fully goes away. The spark of God's purpose for a man never really dies. But for many boys, the challenges of moving into manhood so overwhelm them that they can't hear the call to greatness any more.

To make matters worse, a boy often has few men to step into his life to lead him into noble manhood. That happens, in part, because so few men today have a compelling vision for manhood themselves. As a result, one generation of boys after another enters into manhood confused, lost, frustrated, and resigned, with no anchor to ground them and no vision to drive them.

Created to Save the World

I don't think it's a coincidence that at the same time culture seems to be losing a vision for manhood that superhero movies have exploded onto the big screen: *Batman* and the *Batman* reboots; *Spider-Man* and the *Spider-Man* reboot; *Iron Man*; *Thor*; *Captain America*; *The Hulk*; *The Green Lantern*; *The Avengers*; along with the epic quest movies *The Lord of the Rings*, *Harry Potter*, and *The Hobbit*. These movies speak to the God-given call for boys to grow into heroic men. These movies also provide a boy pictures of what it looks like to live out his destiny: saving the world.

Woven into a boy's DNA by his Creator is a deeply embedded call to make a difference in the world, to build a better world (testosterone is the energy of superheroes). Every time a boy helps someone, every time a boy creates something of beauty, every time a boy builds something, every time a boy expresses anger at what he perceives to be a wrong, every time a boy uses his gifts to serve his neighbor, he is expressing his innate God-given call to save the world.

That call to save the world will more often than not be localized for each boy as he becomes a man: building his family, investing himself in meaningful work, giving money to charity, serving at a homeless kitchen, etc. For that to happen, however, he needs a big, overarching vision of his mission in life—a vision that he can live into; a vision he can see; a vision that calls to him, shapes him, and empowers him to live heroically in his corner of the world.

A Boy After God's Heart

As Saul, Israel's first king, became increasingly incoherent, God began the search for a new king. He sent his prophet Samuel to the house of Jesse, a man who had eight sons. When Samuel met the oldest son, Eliab, he immediately assumed, presumably based on Eliab's height and physical appearance, that he would be the next king. God, however, had a different way of evaluating a man. He told Samuel not to evaluate a man based on his appearance because God looks on the heart (1 Samuel 16:7).

God ended up choosing the youngest of Jesse's sons, David, to be his next king. Something about David's heart suggested he was a king in the making. That something was later defined. David was "a man [a teenage boy at the time!] after God's own heart" (1 Samuel 13:13–14).

Often when we think about David as a boy after God's heart, we think of someone in tune with God. Someone on the same wavelength as God. But the word *after* is a "boy" word, an action word. It means to pursue, to chase—to run after God's heart, do what God wants, and live the life God created us to live.

To say it another way, David's heroic heart was forged by a grace so compelling that he couldn't help but chase after God's heart. He drew his energy from God. He drew his sense of masculinity from God. Responding to God's call on his life, David chased after the heart of God, which in turn forged a noble, heroic spirit in him.

We see that noble, heroic spirit in one of the great boy stories in the Bible. The soldiers of Israel found themselves in a stalemate with the army of the Philistines, who, seeing an opportunity for victory, issued a challenge to the Israelites: a one-on-one fight between the soldier of Israel's choosing and the Philistine solider Goliath. The loser's army would surrender to the winner's army. The problem for the Israelites: Goliath was a giant, and not one Israelite soldier was man enough to fight him.

One day, David went to visit his brothers, who served as Israelite soldiers on the frontlines. While there, he heard Goliath begin his daily taunting and calling out of the Israelite soldiers. When David discovered that none of the Israelites soldiers had the courage to fight the giant, he volunteered to do it himself. He fully trusted that God could beat the giant through him.

Again, not one of the Israelite men stepped up to fight the giant. But David, possibly still a boy or a teenager, his heart forged by chasing after God's heart, did a man's job and beat the giant with one expertly aimed stone to the head. (Goliath's final words, "I never had anything like that enter my mind before!")

David went on to become a powerful soldier, a great leader, and eventually the king of Israel. He lived an honorable, noble, heroic life—a life shaped by the power of God's call on him.

For most of his life, that is. Years later, David took his eye off the ball. He deviated from pursuing the heart of God and lost his way. He ended up committing adultery, ordering the murder of his lover's husband, and almost lost his kingdom to his rebellious son as a result.

However, David still serves as a metaphor for a compelling vision of manhood. He shows us the power a boy experiences when he grows up chasing after the heart of God. But he also reminds us of the mess we can make of our lives when we choose to chase after our own agenda rather than God's.

Over one thousand years after David, Jesus came on the scene, calling a few young men into compelling manhood. He called them to chase after God's heart by following him. As they followed Jesus and responded to his call of grace and chased after his heart, Jesus began to instill a vision in their souls. He took some common, ordinary young men and forged them into men who changed the world.

God forges the spirit of boys through his call of grace on their lives. As boys hear that call and follow Jesus—as they chase after the heart of God—God energizes them with a vision for what it means to be a heroic man and leads them into heroic living. God, however, more often than not, uses people like us—moms, dads, grandpas, grandmas, pastors, youth leaders, and Sunday school teachers—to instill that vision into our boys.

Which leads to the big questions: How do we impart a compelling vision for manhood in our boys? What tools do we have at our disposal? What does a boy/man after God's own heart look like? How do we help our boys hear the call of Jesus in their lives?

Metaphors and Stories

Boys learn visually. Metaphors and stories provide us tools we can use to begin to capture a boy's heart with a compelling vision. Literature and psychology offer us some *visual* metaphors and stories that give boys "pictures," or a vision, of manhood to live into—pictures that Jesus himself modeled.

Example: *The Sword*

In the rite of passage experience that Michael Gurian and I created for junior high boys, *Following Jesus: A Heroic Quest for Boys,* we use the sword as the defining metaphor in the program. Throughout literature, the sword represents a boy's growing power. It serves as a symbol for his superhero powers—his gifts and talents. The sword becomes such an important part of the boy's life and his quest that more often than not he names the sword:

- *Arthur and Excalibur* (this was the sword given to Arthur later in life by the Lady in the Lake, not the sword he pulled out of the stone)

- *Frodo and Sting* (*The Lord of the Rings*)

- *Percy Jackson and Riptide* (*Percy Jackson & the Olympians*)

- *Peter Pevensie and Rhindon* (*The Chronicles of Narnia*)

- *Luke Skywalker* and his light saber (*Star Wars*)

- *Harry Potter* and his wand (which was his sword) plus the sword *Gryffindor*

Crucial to a boy's quest to become a man is learning how to use his sword in good, noble, honorable ways—to use his growing power, gifts, and talents to serve others. Boys are fascinated with swords. We can use that fascination as a metaphor for what it means to be good man. We can give them practical examples of what it looks like to pledge their sword—their allegiance—their lives to the cause of Jesus.

Example: *The Faces of Manhood*

As stated earlier, literature and psychology provide overarching metaphors or archetypes to help guide the boys in what it looks like to use his sword of power heroically. Below are three of the six metaphors we use in *Following Jesus: A Heroic Quest for Boys*:

Prince/King: Living six hours by car from Disneyland, we took our kids to the Happiest Place on Earth at least twice a year. One of the big attractions for our kids back then was *The Sword in the Stone*. At certain times during the day, Merlin would make an appearance, do a short ceremony, and invite a couple of people to try to pull the sword out of the stone. Usually, he would start with a dad standing nearby. No matter how hard Dad pulled, the sword didn't budge. Then Merlin would bring up one of the children. And sure enough, after a few pulls and a few magic words, the child was able to pull the sword out of the stone. And for the rest of that day, that child would be the honorary king (or queen) of Disneyland.

We would always try to get there early to stand as close to Merlin as possible in the hope that one our kids would be chosen. It took countless trips and a period of years, but both our daughter and son pulled the sword from the stone, making them queen and king for the day!

In the legends of King Arthur, baby Arthur, son of Uther-Pendragon, was taken by Merlin to a secret place to protect him from Pendragon's enemies. Merlin then devised a sign whereby England would recognize its true king: a sword in the stone. In gold letters about the sword were written these words, "Whoever pulls this sword out of the anvil is the rightful heir and king of Britain." Merlin promised that the person who pulled the sword from the stone would be wiser and greater and more worthy of praise than even Uther-Pendragon.

Years later, young Arthur did what no one else before him could do—he pulled the sword from the stone—proving he had a king's heart.

Howard Pyle, in writing the story of Arthur, says this about the face of a king:

> When a man is king above men, as was King Arthur, then is he of such a calm and equal temper that neither victory nor defeat may cause him to become either unduly exalted in his own opinion or so troubled in spirit as to be altogether cast down into despair … Yea, he who is true king of men, will not say to himself, "Lo! I am worthy to be crowned with laurels"; but rather he will say to himself, "What ore is there that I may do to make the world the better because of my endeavors?"[2]

The *Prince/King* captures the leadership spirit of a boy, a man-in-the-making. He leads by serving others. He leads by seeking the best in others. He leads by using his sword—his gifts and talents—to make the world a better place. He seeks to do the right thing rather than giving in to peer pressure. He takes responsibility for his actions rather than blaming others. He does his homework and his chores without complaining. He keeps his commitments. He hangs out with a buddy who seems to be upset. He tells the truth. He acts compassionately toward his siblings. As he moves into manhood, he learns to bless those around him with goodness, compassion, and strength. He brings calm and stability to his area of influence. He acts courageously and always stands on the side of the powerless. He makes his family a priority. He takes time off work to catch his son's basketball game. He works hard to provide financially for his family. He constantly affirms and compliments those he cares about. A heroic boy is a superhero with a prince's heart.

Jesus modeled the *King* face throughout his entire ministry. He blessed people by healing them and feeding them. He brought calm in the midst of chaos (i.e., on the boat in the midst of the storm, in the face of a demon-filled madman). He stood against bullies who victimized those who couldn't fight for themselves. He brought justice, grace, and forgiveness to his subjects. He used his sword of power to bring goodness and life to those under his leadership.

An important part of noble manhood is learning to lead—to use one's sword—like a benevolent king, a king with a father's heart. A king like Arthur—wise, good, noble, and focused on others. A king like Jesus. A king in touch with the full range of his emotions and knowing how to express them appropriately. A king who has developed a healthy emotional language.

Jesus invites boys to follow him as their king. As they do, he will forge in them the spirit of a king who can pull his sword from the stone and use it in the service of Jesus.

Stories of fictional kings, biblical kings, and modern-day men living out the *King* face in their jobs and families, give boys pictures of what it looks like to be a good man. And stories of tyrant kings and weak, self-serving kings give boys images to steer clear of in their lives.

Warrior: A warrior never gives up. A warrior keeps going. He faces challenges with courage. He fights for causes he believes in. He acknowledges fear in his life—but refuses to let that fear rule him. He pledges his warrior's sword to the cause of Jesus, using his strengths to bring grace to the world. While at times he may have to fight to destroy something evil or wrong in order to give life, the primary use of his sword is life-giving.

> *We need warriors today, not for fighting each other but for fighting hunger, discrimination, pollution, human slavery, and the abduction of children for soldiery, among many other conditions of human and animal suffering. We need warriors who can battle cogently and convincingly in boardrooms and in the media, in schools and courtrooms, in forgotten jail cells and in dusty fields long rendered infertile by poverty, pollution, or civil war. And we need leaders among these warriors who can match the nuanced complexions of these kinds of battles with an incisive intelligence, stellar communication skills, and a talent for moving fluidly between competing perspectives and entities.*[3]

Think Frodo and Samwise as they near the fires of Mount Doom. Frodo has lost his warrior spirit. Samwise, his friend, yells at him, "I may not be able to carry the ring for you, Mr. Frodo, but I can carry you." Samwise taps into his warrior spirit and carries Frodo to the top of the mountain.

Think Kurt Warner, NFL quarterback. Kurt went to two Super Bowls with the Saint Louis Rams only to be traded to the New York Giants and then quickly benched in favor of Eli Manning. From there, he was traded to the Arizona Cardinals, the NFL's most inept franchise. I know—I'm a season ticket holder and a long-suffering fan. Once again, he sat on the bench. No one believed he had it any more. But Kurt didn't give up. He moved himself into the starting QB position and led the Cardinals to their first ever Super Bowl appearance, playing one of the greatest games in Super Bowl history.

During that game, he led his team back from a deficit to take the lead with two and half minutes left, only to lose in the final seconds. I know—I was there. Kurt models the warrior spirit.

Think David versus Goliath. Harry Potter versus Lord Voldemort. Percy Jackson versus the "bad guy" Greek gods. The Knights of the Round Table:

> The Round Table was established with great pomp and ceremony of estate … Then all the knights arose, and each knight held up before him the cross of the hilt of his sword, and each knight spake word for word as King Arthur spake. And this was the covenant of their Knighthood of the Round Table: That they would be gentle unto the weak; that they would be courageous unto the strong; that they would be terrible unto the wicked and the evil-doer; that they would defend the helpless who should call upon them for aid; that all women should be held unto them sacred; that they would stand unto the defence of one another whensoever such defence should be required; that they would be merciful unto all men; that they would be gentle of deed, true in friendship, and faithful in love. This was their covenant, and unto it each knight sware upon the cross of his sword, and in witness thereof did kiss the hilt thereof.[4]

Imagine a generation of that kind of warrior-spirit-infused boys!

Jesus lived out his warrior spirit constantly. He used his "sword of power" to fight against hunger. Sickness. Death. Injustice. Oppression. Hatred. Violence. In the face of horrific death, he kept going. He didn't give up. He didn't run. While acknowledging his fear, he courageously moved to the cross—and he did it for us.

Jesus, through us, is calling our boys to that kind of warrior spirit—a bold, daring, reckless, love-immersed spirit that fights for the cause of Jesus—the cause of bringing grace to the world.

Servant: Ultimately, a good man follows Jesus by serving others—by using his sword to make the world a better place. Jesus came to serve and give his life as a ransom for others. Boys are well on their way to being the men God created them to be when they learn to serve others—to do to others as they would have others do to them. When they learn to go out of their way to help around the house, to help out at school, to serve the community, to serve at church, they discover what it means to be a real man.

Hours before Jesus laid down his life for us on the cross, he modeled servanthood by washing the feet of his disciples. Only the lowliest of lowly servants carried out that job. In Jesus' day, the roads weren't paved. They were often muddy and filled with animal you-know-what and even human you-know-what. Imagine having to wash that stuff off of size twelve feet—big, gross feet with bunions and warts and hair on the toes! Imagine having to scrape that stuff out of every crevice, working between each toe, and wiping off each toe hair! The job was so disgusting and demeaning that most of the time people didn't acknowledge the foot washer.

No wonder the disciples were horrified when Jesus began washing their feet. But Jesus, through his actions, taught a valuable lesson: "This is what it looks like to follow me! This is what a real man looks like! This is what it looks like to use your sword of power!" Another way of saying it is, Jesus calls us to take up the cross—to take up our swords—and follow him. To take up the cross is to follow Jesus back into the world to bring grace to the world.

As boys pledge their swords of power to Jesus and his mission, as they chase after his heart, he forges in them the heart of a *King, Warrior,* and *Servant.*

Superheroes (think Spider-Man: "With great power comes great responsibility"), civic heroes (firefighters, police officers, soldiers, business leaders, teachers), sports analogies, and even video games can provide stories and metaphors for boys that can forge in them a heart after God's heart—a heart set on saving the world.

A life-affirming, compelling vision for manhood provides part of the package for forging the spirit of boys and changing the storyline of their lives. But boys also need something that equips and empowers them to follow Jesus into heroic manhood. They need a strategy.

5

An Empowering Strategy for Life

> *Today's young men are coming of age in an era with no road maps, no blueprints, and no primers to tell them what a man is or how to become one.[1]*

December 11, 1973: A cold winter day in Minneapolis, Minnesota. A school day. But not an ordinary school day—at least not for me. Sixteen years after my mom had given birth to me, the moment school let out, my dad picked me up to take me to my behind-the-wheel driver's test. We headed to a testing site in Plymouth, just outside of Minneapolis.

If I remember right, I took the test in our yellow AMC Hornet. The instructor sat on the passenger's side with clipboard in hand and told me to drive. Throughout the drive, I was instructed to perform several different tasks: parallel parking, parking on a hill, make a left turn, stops, etc. After each task, the instructor made a note on the clipboard. Finally, he told me to pull up next to the curb in front of the main building. I parked. I turned off the car. He opened the door to check my parking job. He shut the door. He put a big line through some number. Then he turned to me and said, "I thought you were going to be my first perfect score. But you parked two feet away from the curb just now and lost four points out of one hundred!"

Moments later, I was driving home with my driver's license.

When we got home, I asked Dad if I could go out for a while. He gave me the keys, and I officially entered a new phase of life—that of an independent driver. All these years later, I can still remember that first drive of freedom and how great it felt to move a step deeper into manhood—being able to get around without Mom's or Dad's help.

Getting a driver's license is one of the few intentional rites of passage left in our culture.

Rites of Passage

> *In the United States, proving masculinity appears to be a lifelong project, endless and unrelenting. Daily, grown men call each other out, challenging one another's manhood. And it works most of the time. You can pretty much guarantee starting a fight virtually anywhere in America by questioning someone's manhood. But why must guys test and prove their masculinity so obsessively? Why are the stakes so high? Why so different here than elsewhere? In part, it's because the transitional moment itself is so ill-defined. We, as a culture, lack any coherent ritual that might demarcate the passage from childhood to adulthood for men or women. Not surprisingly, it also remains unclear who, exactly, has the authority to do the validating.[2]*

A rite of passage is an intentional period of training involving instruction, tasks, mentoring, some sort of public "test," and a ceremony celebrating the accomplishments of the passage. The point of the passage varies, but generally, the purpose is to guide and equip someone to move from one phase of life to the next. In the case of driving, I took classroom training, behind-the-wheel instruction, a written test, spent several hours driving with Mom or Dad, and then took the final driving test. It all culminated with the awarding of a driver's license and the ultimate ceremony—being handed the keys to the car for the very first time. In that rite of passage, I transitioned from a dependent passenger to an independent driver. I moved from little responsibility to great responsibility. But I wasn't left to figure it out on my own. I went through a systematic process that equipped me for the responsibilities I was about to take on as a driver.

Throughout history, cultures all around the world have intuited the need for boys to go through a rite of passage to prepare them for manhood. This intuited need for a rite of passage shows itself in the great heroic quest stories throughout history. Each of these stories, at the root level, is a story about a boy going through the passage from boyhood to manhood: facing impossible tasks; mentored by a wise man or men; grappling with success and failure; facing his deepest fears; persevering through the quest; and ultimately accomplishing his goal—a goal celebrated by his friends and mentors. And when he looks back, he sees that he is no longer a boy but a man in the making—and a heroic man at that. Think:

- *Frodo and Samwise,* on a quest to destroy the One Ring— guided by Gandalph and Aragorn, facing insurmountable odds, evil, and fear, calling on reserves within themselves they didn't know they had, and ultimately destroying the ring on Mount Doom;

- *Harry Potter,* over the course of seven years, discovering his growing power as a boy and its right and wrong uses, guided by Dumbledore, battling one impossible challenge after another, facing unimaginable fears, and ultimately destroying Lord Voldemort, becoming a heroic man in the process;

- *Percy Jackson,* fighting against the Titans to save the gods of Olympus, not only discovering his true identity along the way, but also becoming a man in the making; and

- *Peter Pevensie,* guided by Aslan, facing one adventure after another in the battle to save Narnia, becoming a king as a result.

All of these stories and many more capture the need boys have to go through a rite of passage—a process that guides them into and equips them for noble manhood.

Girls have a monthly, natural, biological rite of passage that moves them into womanhood. Boys don't have that. Certainly things start happening to a boy physically that tips him off that he is moving into new territory:

- His voice begins to deepen.

- His complexion changes.

- He begins to develop a more muscular physique.

- He may begin to withdraw from parents and spend more time with friends or hide out alone in his cave. The openness and perhaps even hugs and kisses he shared with his parents may diminish.

- He experiences mood swings ranging from giddiness to anger to seeming depression—all in the span of thirty seconds!

These changes, however, don't necessarily infuse his spirit with a noble view of manhood. Boys have no nature-based reminder of impending adulthood calling them up into honorable adulthood.

Our ancestors, including our biblical ancestors, understood that. While they may not have known about testosterone and its effect on boys, they knew what it did to boys. They knew intuitively, as have many tribal cultures throughout history, that boys need men to mentor them during adolescence—men who will help these testosterone-charged boys harness their aggression and energy for good, noble, honorable purposes. If left without guidance, these boys could too easily end up using their energy selfishly and destructively. To help them, culture after culture throughout history created rites of passages for boys, the purpose of which was to help the boys turn:

- their aggression toward service to the community

- their competitive nature toward compassion

- their high-risk urges toward a meaningful purpose in life

A rite of passage provides a significant structured experience that moves the boy through the transition from boyhood to manhood. It involves mentoring along with challenging tasks to help the boy discover what it means to be a good man. It gives a boy the chance to slow down as he grows up in order for the tribe/community/church and family to instill in him healthy morals and belief systems that will lead him into manhood. A rite of passage empowers parents and elders to raise their sons into noble men. Without it, boys will make up their own definitions of manhood, lean on each other to determine what it means to be a man, and create their own rites for proving their manhood (i.e., hazings, binge drinking, and hooking up in college).

Many Native American tribes put boys through years of rites of passage. Jewish boys participate in rigorous study and performance experiences leading to their bar mitzvah. Similarly, among the Greeks and Byzantines, boys were required to perform spiritual tasks for an extended period of time in order to become Christian adults.

Today, with a few exceptions, our twenty-first century, US culture has all but abandoned this important aspect of adolescence. As a result, our boys, looking for a meaningful vision of manhood, look for guidance in other places, mainly their friends and media. Media, in particular, paints a picture of manhood based on consumerism, gratification, the self at all costs, and a lack of responsibility. All too often, boys end up lost in terms of a defining vision of what it means to be a man, which leads to what some experts are now calling a crisis of "permanent adolescence"—boys in men's bodies.

> *Twenty-four percent of students involved in church groups were subjected to hazing activities, and more than a third said they didn't tell anyone about it because "there is no one to tell" or "adults won't handle it right."*[3]

Confirmation and Rites of Passage

Many denominations and congregations offer their youth an experience called confirmation. Generally, confirmation targets kids—boys and girls together—in junior high. Confirmation "confirms" the faith of the students by taking them through an intensive period of study that focuses on the Bible, church history (we Lutherans, for example, review the life of Martin Luther and the Protestant Reformation), and church theology (baptism/communion). Confirmation provides a Christian framework for life. The hope and prayer is that the students will move from embracing the faith of their parents to owning the faith themselves. At the end of the confirmation program, the students are publically "confirmed" in a celebration at church. (I attended an Evangelical Free Church when in junior high. We didn't have a confirmation program per se. Instead, we had a similar program with similar outcomes called the "Pastor's Instruction Class." We met for two hours every Saturday for two years.)

In a sense, confirmation serves as a type of a rite of passage, as it includes instruction and tasks to be performed (homework, missions projects, memory verses, etc.) and culminates with a ceremony marking this new stage of life—moving from the faith of childhood to the faith of an adult. In some congregations, confirmed students become full members of the church, meaning, in part, that they are able to vote.

There are important differences, however, between a confirmation program and a rite of passage:[4]

Rite of Passage	*Confirmation*
The overarching question:	
What kind of a man do you want to be?	*What do you believe?*
The driving force:	
Calling a boy into manhood	*Confirming one's faith*
The starting point:	
A vision for manhood shaped by Jesus	*The Christian faith story*

The end result:

Living out the vision for manhood   Understanding one's faith

The students:

Boys   Boys and girls together

Mentors:

Crucial—men only   Optional—men or women

A confirmation-type experience is vitally important for the faith development of boys and girls. A rite of passage is absolutely crucial for the faith and manhood development of boys in the twenty-first century (and increasingly for girls as well). The world needs men living a compelling vision of Christian manhood (and women living a compelling vision of Christian womanhood). The best of all worlds would be to offer both a rite of passage and a confirmation program.

Two Rites of Passage Examples:
Example 1—Following Jesus: A Heroic Quest for Boys

When Michael Gurian and I started talking about how the church could better impact and captivate boys, it didn't take long to get to rites of passage. Michael's book, *The Purpose of Boys*, articulates a passion and plan for taking boys through such an experience as they begin to move into adolescence. Using that book, Michael's experiences with bar mitzvahs, and my background as a pastor, we began to talk about what a twenty-first century Christian rite of passage might look like. My passion was to create a tool that would help congregations and dads disciple their boys, i.e., call boys into and equip them for a manhood shaped by Jesus. So we created a program called *Following Jesus: A Heroic Quest for Boys.* The fundamental question shaping this rite of passage is, What does it look like to follow Jesus into manhood?

Michael's book provided the foundation. Using the word *heroic* as an acronym and the story of Joseph as a metaphor, Michael laid out six qualities of a heroic man:

- honorable

- enterprising

- responsible

- original

- intimate

- creative

I then added the metaphors gleaned from psychology and literature:

- *Honorable King*—one who does the right thing and blesses those in his circle of influence

- *Enterprising Warrior*—one who never gives up and who uses his "sword of power" to fight for what is right, just, and life-giving

- *Responsible Servant*—committed to serving others

- *Original Craftsman*—created as God's masterpiece for good works, using his gifts and talents in the service of Jesus

- *Intimate Friend*—one who loves others as Jesus loves and who treats all people with dignity and respect

- *Creative Explorer*—one who lives his life creatively exploring the depths of God's profound grace and love

From there I, along with Michael's input, created seven interactive sessions that introduced the boys and their mentors to each of the six HEROIC character qualities. The sessions include Bible stories, games, video clips, competitions, and current stories. Each of those sessions is followed up by a small-group experience the next week. Each small group is made up of the boy and his two to three mentors (one of whom is dad). The small groups, with guided questions that we wrote, dig deeper into each HEROIC quality and personalizes it for each mentor and boy. A weekend retreat, a service project, and a few "Quest Tasks" rounds out the program.

The "Quest" culminates in two celebrations. The first is for the boys and their families and friends, where each boy presents his "Jesus Project" (one of his tasks). The second celebration takes place in front of the congregation. The boy reads a passage from Mark (one of the tasks of the Quest is to read through Mark and note how Jesus lived out the HEROIC qualities). He is then blessed, prayed for, given a Bible, and presented as a man to the worshipping community.

Throughout the entire process, the boys are constantly asked the questions:

- What kind of man do you want to be?

- What does it look like to follow Jesus into manhood?

- What does it look like for you to pledge your sword of power to the service of Jesus?

Through the big sessions, the small groups, the HEROIC tasks, and the retreat, the boys receive insights, male energy, and practical biblical and life insights to help them answer those questions heroically.

*Example 2—**Marking Transitions***

Robert Lewis, in his book *Raising a Modern-Day Knight* and the program based on the book, talks about marking transitions in a boy's life with a ceremony as a type of rite of passage. For example, when a boy graduates from high school, mark the occasion with a ceremony. The ceremony can include some sort of teaching/mentoring about this next phase of manhood, a gift marking the event (i.e., a plaque, a ring, etc.), and a celebration (a meal, for example.)

Inspired by the concept, I created a ceremony for my son, Mike, to celebrate the birth of his first child. I went over to his house, unannounced, and asked him to lunch. (My son hates surprises, so his first response was one of alarm, "What's wrong?" It took several minutes before his adrenaline settled down.) We headed over to my dad's house for some of his world-famous chili (famous in our world, anyway). Waiting for us were my dad, Mike's father-in-law, my brother, and a man who had been a mentor to Mike. We sat at the table, "chewing the fat," and then moved into the living room.

One by one, each of the men read a letter to Mike that I had asked them to prepare ahead of time. In the letter, they talked about what they had learned as dads that they wanted to pass along to him and included a word of blessing for Mike. We then prayed for him and took pictures.

After that, Mike and I jumped into the car for the next surprise. I had scheduled an appointment for us to get matching tattoos to "mark" the ceremony. The artist designed a "Fatherhood" tattoo for us with a crown (king), sword (warrior), heart (lover), and cross (servant). Underneath, we put the birthdates of our kids—in Mike's case, the birth date of his daughter, Clover.

To top off the ceremony, I gave Mike a journal that I had written (in my own hard-to-read handwriting) over the span of several weeks. It told my story, the story of my dad, and the story of my relationship with Mike, along with some words of wisdom and blessing I wanted to pass on to him.

Mike's not a highly emotional guy (except at football games), but I could tell in the way he talked about the ceremony to my wife that night that it was deeply moving to him. The brief e-mail he sent me after he read my journal confirmed it. My wife sealed the deal by putting a picture book together of the entire ceremony.

The Key to a High-Impact Rite of Passage: Mentors

As noted before, in the great quest stories throughout history, every boy, when called into a quest, found himself surrounded by mentors to guide him. King Arthur had Merlin. Frodo had Gandalph. The disciples had Jesus. Harry Potter had Dumbledore. Timothy had Paul. Boys need male energy and wisdom from other men in order to navigate the move into manhood successfully.

In the twenty-first century, the overwhelming majority of boys are being mentored primarily by women: moms and grandmas, female preschool teachers, female elementary teachers, female Sunday school teachers, and, more often than not, educational TV shows skewed to girls. A few fortunate boys have a dad, uncle, or grandpa to pour male energy into the boy. For far too many boys, however, Dad no longer lives at home, is disengaged even though he does live at home, or feels inadequate to strategically raise his son into manhood. Like Tom Sawyer, who was raised by his aunt Polly (who did her best) and Huck Finn, whose dad was an alcoholic, many of our boys have no strong, male role models in their lives.

Boys need men to teach them how to be men. Boys know intuitively that men validate them as men. As boys start moving into fourth grade, they increasingly need male energy poured into them. They need to see from other men what it looks like to live like an honorable friend, husband, worker, neighbor, student, and so on. They need a variety of men to mentor them so that they see several pictures of Christian manhood. (That's why we encourage three mentors in our rite of passage program.) A manhood vision can only be transferred to a boy via a man. Boys need their moms. They need the influence of women. But they need men to make them men.

Congregations can provide a transforming gift to families and boys in the form of mentors. Every congregation has men sitting on the sidelines looking for something significant and "manly" to do with their lives. Many of those men, through a compelling vision and the tools to carry out that vision, would be honored to mentor boys.

My experience with our rite of passage program is that dads want to mentor their sons. They want to shape their lives. They just simply feel inadequate to do so.

The genius of Michael's book, *The Purpose of Boys*, centers on equipping dads to mentor their sons. In our Quest program, Dad is the primary mentor. We provide everything he needs to successfully mentor his son. While leading the boys into manhood, we are leading dads into dadhood—empowering and equipping dads to pass along heroic, Christ-centered, male energy to their sons. (If there is no dad in the family, we provide help in recruiting a father figure because every boy needs a father figure in his life.)

Imagine what could happen in your congregation if you:

- provided a clear path to Christ-centered manhood for your boys

- empowered and equipped dads to mentor their sons

- invited, empowered, and equipped the men in your congregation to pour male energy into the boys in your congregation

While a three-month, intensive rite of passage can't make a boy into a man, it can give him the foundation he needs to start thinking about his life, his life choices, and the kind of man he wants to be. More importantly, it creates a new bond between father and son, a bond forged as the two of them hear the call of Jesus to follow him. It also connects him to mentors to whom he can turn again and again for guidance, wisdom, and support as he makes his journey into manhood.

Look at what Jesus did with eleven disciples! We can literally change the world by changing the storyline of our boys, their dads, and the men in our churches. For that to happen, however, each congregation will have to do something courageous: reshape itself to become a boy friendly church.

Part 3

Forging the Spirit of Your Congregation:
A Church for Boys

6

Speaking "Boy"

> The three children set out for Sunday School—a place Tom hated with his whole heart; but Sid and Mary were fond of it.[1]

Tom's parents decide to visit a new church. They force Tom, almost against his will, to go to the Sunday school class offered during worship. Tom reluctantly walks into the Sunday school room, but it's no ordinary room. His jaw drops as he moves into a mostly dark hall—a cross between a concert club and a video arcade. Loud music blasts from speakers located throughout the room while fast-moving videos flash across TV monitors also scattered around the hall. Off to the left hangs a huge metal circular contraption with seven video game monitors attached. At least forty boys crowd around, watching and waiting their turn to play. Off to the right is a food bar with cola machines, snacks, and pizza.

At nine a.m., a band jumps on stage and begins to lead the kids in several high-energy praise songs. Once the singing is done, the leader calls a few kids onto the stage for a messy, gooey competition while the kids in the audience choose a team to cheer for. Another high-energy song by the band and then the leader talks to the kids about some guy named David who fought a giant with a slingshot, killed him, and then lopped off his head with the giant's own sword.

Tom runs out of Sunday school and can't stop talking about it to his parents. The next Saturday night, he begs his parents to take him to church on Sunday. He even takes a Saturday night bath without complaining. Sunday school is the best fifty minutes of his week.

Tom's parents decide to visit a new church. They force Tom, almost against his will, to go to the Sunday school class offered during worship. Tom reluctantly walks into the Sunday school room. Ten chairs circle a table. One chair sits empty—between two girls. The only other boy sits off in the corner by himself, refusing to join the group. An old lady—about forty—and her daughter lead the class. They seem nice enough.

The teacher hands out Bibles to each of the students and has them turn to 1 Samuel 17. Tom has no idea what that means or where to find it. Becky, the girl next to him, sighs, opens his Bible for him to the right place, and points to the passage. The teacher then asks the students to take turns reading the story, one verse per person. Tom immediately tenses up. He doesn't read well out loud. The girls read flawlessly. Tom stumbles several times, and a couple of the girls begin to giggle. The story seems like it could be pretty cool, but Tom is so embarrassed by his performance that he barely pays attention.

The teacher reads something to the class that has to do with the story and what it means for their lives. Tom begins to fidget. The other boy fidgets in the corner as well. The teacher politely asks them to sit quietly while she finishes the lesson.

After what seems like three hours, the teacher wraps up her lesson and says that they will now do something fun. *Finally!* Tom thinks to himself. The teacher hands out crayons and a blank sheet of paper and asks the students to draw a picture that captures the point of the story they just looked at. Tom groans. He hates drawing. He stares at the paper while the girls around him dive in and create imaginative and beautiful representations of the story. Tom finally draws a stick figure of a giant and a stick figure of David.

Each of the students shows off his or her art. Tom is overwhelmed at the detailed and colorful artwork of the girls. He refuses to show his picture, but the teacher gently forces him to do so to the laughter of the girls in the room.

It was the longest fifty minutes of his life. The following Saturday night, he comes down with a stomachache that he assures his folks will feel better by Monday morning. They'd best go to church without him tomorrow.

Church culture tends to believe that these are the only two options for boys today. The first option is a high-energy, high-cost, staff-intensive experience with a huge "wow" factor for boys. For most congregations, this option is completely out of reach. The second option is "This is the best we can do with what we've got" Sunday school experience. For most congregations, this is our reality. We don't have huge budgets. We don't have the highly skilled staff necessary to pull off high-energy, boy friendly weekly events. We have busy, caring, but not terribly well-equipped volunteers who do their best to try to lead Sunday school each weekend. The classrooms are small, and the classes may be small as well. We buy the best material we can find, but the curriculums tend to favor girl brains. Each Sunday, we have this sinking feeling that we are losing our boys. But what can we do?

The good news is that, with some small tweaks, we can almost immediately up the boy effectiveness with little to no money. Even the smallest of congregations can have a huge impact on boys. In fact, truth be told, the bells and whistles of the high-energy program, while attractive to boys, can sometimes hide the lack of an effective strategy for forging the spirit of boys into heroic men. It may entertain them. It may engage them. But it may not empower them to follow Jesus into manhood.

Whether yours is a congregation pursuing boys through the big, high-energy event or a congregation struggling to pull off Sunday school each week let alone reach boys, learning the art of speaking "boy" can energize your church to forge the spirit of boys with the power of grace.

An important note before proceeding: Below and in the next chapter I will advocate for men to teach boys, especially as boys move into fourth grade. However, men and women can use the "boy speak" ideas I list below regardless of the age of boys. While boys need male leaders, women who speak "boy" can have a profound impact on boys as well. Many of these ideas will work in a boy-girl classroom, enhancing the experience for the boys and the girls.

(Tom) entered the church, now, with a swarm of clean and noisy boys and girls, proceeded to his seat and started a quarrel with the first boy that came in handy. The teacher, a grave, elderly man, interfered; then turned his back a moment and Tom pulled a boy's hair in the next bench, and was absorbed in his book when the boy turned around; stuck a pin in another boy, presently, in order to hear him say "Ouch!" and got a new reprimand from his teacher. Tom's whole class were of a pattern—restless, noisy, and troublesome.[2]

Key #1 to Speaking "Boy": Action!

Contemporary observers of child behavior have documented differences in female and male motor development, noting, among other things, the earlier development of fine motor capacities in preschool and primary grade girls and the tendency of boys the same age to prefer large-muscle activity—running, jumping, riding vehicles; a tendency generally to what the developmental theorist Erik Erickson called, "intrusive play."[3]

Boys are walking volcanoes of testosterone. That testosterone will either explode in bored fidgeting and troublemaking or it can be harnessed as a tool for discipleship and learning.

Boys learn best when the learning is active. Boys bond with others through movement and activity, whereas girls tend to bond through conversation. Connect the lesson to action and the boys will lock in.

Want to engage boys? Do stuff. Move. Compete. Build.

After David Murrow spoke at our church about boys, we did two things immediately. First, we separated the boys from the girls starting in third grade (more on this below), and second, we added in action.

We almost always start the boy's Grace Adventure Club (what we call Sunday school at our church) with some kind of activity. Living in the desert Southwest, we can go outside most Sunday mornings. The boys head out with their male teacher (more on this below) and shoot buckets or play a round of football. Lately, thanks to one of our men who grew up in Australia, Rugby has been the rage. Those ten minutes of play time help the boys run off a bit of testosterone, gets them moving, and enables them to bond with the teacher and the other boys. (When it gets too hot to be outside, we use high-movement indoor games.) It also provides a crucial element for speaking "boy"—fun!

The boys head back into class for a brief lesson presentation by the teacher followed by an activity that helps them connect with the story. Perhaps they will make a slingshot like David's and sling marshmallows at a Goliath. Or build a model rocket as a way to talk about prayer (shooting our prayers up to heaven.) Or create "stone" tablets for the Ten Commandments. Or build a pyramid as a part of the Moses story. Or write and illustrate a comic book on a Bible story. Or design a game board based on a Jesus story. Or use Legos to build a Jesus boat. Or bake manna. Or produce a radio show. Or write song lyrics based on the lesson. While the boys work on their projects, the leaders engage them in conversation about the lesson, school, or sports because boys learn best when they are moving or working on something.

Depending on the length of the lesson and activity, the boys may head back outside for another round of basketball or Rugby.

Sometimes the group never gets to the lesson because they get caught up playing. Because the bonding time through play is so vital to the overall effectiveness of the Grace Adventure Club, it's okay to miss a lesson occasionally. I want our boys to see Christian men in a variety of settings. Missing a lesson once in a while to let the boys play with Christian men is an important part of speaking "boy" and forging the spirit of boys.

As I stated above, action opens boys up to talk. Something about moving or working with their hands loosens up their tongues. That in part is why it's good to discuss a lesson or talk about a boy's life while the boy is doing something.

One of the challenges my leaders wrestled with had to do with getting boys to participate in the lesson discussion. We used great questions (I know because I wrote them!) with little to no response from the boys. So I asked my friend Kathy Stevens from the Gurian Institute if she had any suggestions on how to liven up the discussion. She gave me a simple but profound idea. She suggested that we hand each boy a small pad of paper and a pen. Each time a question was asked, the boys were first given a chance to write down some answers. It worked brilliantly, in part because it offered the boys a chance to internalize their thinking before speaking and because it provided a small form of movement—writing—which helped stimulate their thinking. I now use this simple technique when I'm teaching men as well.

Because boys learn through action, they need lots of space. You may find that some of the discipline problems ease by moving the boys into a larger room. Smaller rooms make them feel confined, which causes them to fidget and act out all the more. Some teachers report that having the boys stand during a brief lecture time can help hold their attention.

I want to reiterate that this does not mean that we should never expect boys to sit still or be quiet. They have a great capacity for sitting quietly (watch, for example, how they sit through an engaging movie—where there is movement on the screen). But congregations committed to captivating boys will take seriously the testosterone surging through boys' bodies and use methods to keep them moving and engaged.

A few other ideas for putting action into learning:

- *Role-play.* Have the boys act out a Bible story. Once during worship, I had the kids come up front. I told the story of Jesus walking on water. As I did so, I gave them directions for acting out the story. When I got to the part about the storm, I had the kids sway back and forth while looking scared. Then

I pulled out a squirt gun and sprayed them with "waves" of water. The boys, in particular, loved that! (One boy ad-libbed and pretended to vomit over the side of the boat.) Have the boys reenact Gideon's battle of the "jars." Or have the boys imagine they are a Bible character and talk about what the character might have been thinking—"What do you think was going on in Judas' mind when he decided to betray Jesus?" Or "Imagine sitting next to Daniel as he tries to figure out if he should pray publically, which could put him in the lion's den, or if he should pray privately, which would spare his life but deny his faith in God."

- *Surprise.* Do something unexpected. Something with a hint of danger or even grossness. For example, when the boys walk into class, be lying down on your side and tell them the story of Ezekiel doing the same to make a point to the Jews (Ezekiel 4). Or, using a slingshot, "pelt" the boys with very soft foam "rocks" or marshmallows as they walk into class in order to set up the story of David and Goliath. Let's face it—anything that captivates and holds a boy's attention during Sunday school will be a pleasant surprise!

- *Create "movement breaks."* Keep the teaching segments to about five to seven minutes and break them up with some sort of brief movement. It can be anything from stretching to five push-ups to a thumb war with another boy. Sixty seconds of movement can help recapture their attention.

Key #2 to Speaking "Boy": Make it Visual

Boys engage best with pictures, object lessons, and metaphors. God wired them to be visual learners. Video clips can help drive home the point of a story or lesson. Dropping eggs on the floor can illustrate the damage we do with our words—how we can break someone's heart or even break a friendship. A water balloon fight can serve as a tie-in to water and baptism.

Sometimes men (or the teachers) can make themselves the object lesson. We spent a few weeks looking at fishing stories from the life of Jesus. One weekend, I had one of our men bring his little fishing boat to church for the boys to jump around on. The next week, another of our men brought some fishing gear and taught the boys how to cast. (I recognized that Jesus' disciples used nets rather than poles, so we showed a picture of how the disciples fished). During a series on heroes, we had some of our men come to class dressed in their work clothes to talk about their jobs (for example: a firefighter and a police officer). The more visual the lesson, the better.

While some boys find it hard to read and to read out loud, we want to instill in them a passion for reading. One way to get the boys to read a Bible story is to make several copies of the story and cut them into puzzle pieces. Depending on the length of the story, the pieces may be sentences, paragraphs, or even a few words. Put the boys into teams, and have them piece together the story puzzle. The first team to complete the puzzle wins the prize.

By the way, seeing men read, and especially seeing men read the Bible, can demonstrate to boys that reading is not girly but manly!

Bible stories, being visual, work best for boys, as they involve boys' imagination. As the story is read (or as the boys read the story), they see it in their heads. The more teaching-oriented Scriptures (i.e., Paul's letters) can be reinforced with object lessons.

Key #3 to Speaking "Boy": Separate the Boys from the Girls

During a Newcomer Orientation, a woman asked why we segregate the boys from the girls. I thanked her for her loaded question with a smile and gave my response. We separate boys from the girls for several reasons (many of which I've already covered in this book):

- *Boys and girls learn differently.* We want to provide an environment for our boys *and* our girls that enables them to learn according to how God has wired their brains. We know boys and girls respond to following Jesus differently, and we want to respect those differences. At the same time, we want to focus the call of Jesus so that boys hear it in boy language and girls hear it in girl language.

- *Girls tend to be ahead of boys in reading and verbal skills.* This embarrasses the boys and frustrates the girls. Separating them enables the leaders to teach to the developmental level of the boys and the girls.

- *Boys need "boy space" to talk about boy stuff.* They need an environment where they can talk freely about their lives without feeling embarrassed by girls. (Girls need the same kind of environment where they can talk about girl stuff without "those boys" snickering at them.)

- *Boys need men to lead them.* As boys start moving into fourth or fifth grade, they increasingly need male energy poured into them. Primarily educated by women and often raised primarily by Mom or Grandma, boys need men in their lives. A Sunday school program can provide one of those places for male mentoring where boys can hang out with men to see what men look like, how they act, and how they follow Jesus. A wise youth leader will provide places for junior and senior high boys to connect with men of all ages to get a feel for what it means to be a Christian man. Getting men to step up and lead Sunday school can prove difficult, as many men feel inadequate for such a task. If we want men to lead, we need to make sure we give them everything they need to lead effectively. That means *everything* from what to say, to what to do, to when to do it, etc. A clearly prepared curriculum can help men win when it comes to teaching our boys.

When I was in sixth grade, Fred led our class. We loved Fred because he loved us, and we knew he was committed to us. And he spoke "boy." Fred would often commit a Saturday to taking us on outings simply to hang with us and pour male energy into us (although he may not have said it that way). During Sunday school, he would listen to our stories and do his best to make the lesson interesting. We loved going to Sunday school because of Fred. To be honest, I can't remember much about what he taught us after all these years, but I remember Fred. I know he was a man of God. In him, I saw a man modeling what it means to follow Jesus. That's the most important lesson a man can pass on to a boy.

Over the last few years, I have cultivated a group of men to work with our boys. I made a commitment to them that I would pour myself into them so they could pour themselves into our boys and promised that I would make them "boy experts." I purchased a copy of *The Purpose of Boys* for each of the men, and we meet once a month or so to talk about the book, about boys in general, about the boys we are leading, and how we can better call boys to follow Jesus.

This does not mean women should step aside and no longer invest in boys. Boys need good female role models as well. They need to see how women respond to life and faith so that the boys can learn to live in healthy relationships with women. Boys also need the gifts and insights that women bring to life. But again, because they are men in the making, boys need men to lead them to manhood—men like Fred who have the courage to look boys in the eyes and say, "Follow me as I follow Jesus!"

Key #4 to Speaking "Boy": Engage Boys Emotionally

This may seem counterintuitive to much of what I have written. Boys tend to have difficulty expressing emotions. Because their boy brain doesn't connect thought/experience to emotion like a girl brain does, boys find it harder to talk about their feelings. On top of that, boy/man culture often encourages boys to "man-up" and squelch their emotions: "Big boys don't cry. Suck it up. Tough it out."

Surprisingly, research tells us that boys are actually more emotionally vulnerable than girls (see Dan Kindlon's and Michael Thompson's excellent book *Raising Cain: Protecting the Emotional Life of Boys*). Boys do feel things deeply, but they often lack the emotional language to express those feelings. Or they are afraid they will look girly if they express their emotions. Often, the only time boys/men are free to express a wide variety of emotions is when they are watching sports. During a three-hour football game, a boy/man will cheer, curse, despair, and cry (either tears of defeat or victory). The same is true when watching a "man movie."

Part of being a heroic man is to be an emotionally healthy man—one who is in tune with his emotions and able to articulate them in appropriate ways. A few suggestions on how to engage boys emotionally:

- *What are you* thinking? *versus What are you* feeling? When trying to get a boy to engage emotionally, rather than asking, "What are you feeling?" try starting with, "What are you thinking?" Boys understand thinking language better than feeling language when it comes to their own stuff or when it comes to the point of a story. "What do you think the character is thinking at that point?" Or to move it to a more emotional level, "Can you remember a time when you felt sad? Or guilty?" and then help the boy connect that emotional moment to the emotional moment a character in the Bible is experiencing. Boys need time to process an emotion into words, so we need to provide that time if we want to know what they are feeling. (You might experiment by having the boy write down a few emotional thoughts or impressions first before talking about them.)

- *Connect emotions with action.* In the twenty-first century, much of Christianity is expressed in highly emotional and feeling-oriented terms. Worship services need to move people emotionally. We're called to love Jesus, often using romantic-type language to describe that love. Love, joy, compassion, kindness, mercy, peace, and grace form the bedrock of the Christian life. But for boys, those words, as often defined in current Christian culture, come across as girly. For Jesus, love, compassion, joy, and grace were emotions, yes, but more than emotions, they were ways of acting. Putting a "Jesus spin" on these words can help call greatness out of our boys. For Jesus:

Love is living a life of sacrifice, commitment, generosity, and service.

Compassion is the motivation to help someone in need. (In Mark's gospel, Jesus' compassion always grew out of his anger at anything that hurt people.)

Joy is living in the certainty of God's commitment to us.

Grace is the reckless action of accepting anyone and everyone.

These emotional words are, for Jesus, action words—emotions put into the service of helping others. We want to call boys to follow Jesus, not to feeling a certain way about him. We want to invite boys to look at how they interact with Jesus not only on the basis of how they feel about him or on how he makes them feel, but on how they are living the life he called them to live.

- *Lead emotionally.* We want to help our boys learn to process their emotions in healthy ways (not in the stereotypical male way of keeping them bottled up). We want to teach our boys that Jesus showed his emotions openly. He wept at the tomb of his friend Lazarus. When he saw the leper, he was moved with compassion—a deep-seated anger that stirred in him over the horror that the leper was experiencing—a stirring that people could see. Jesus showed a sense of fear in Gethsemane, sweating drops of blood (a form of shock). Jesus was not afraid of emotions or of showing them. Neither should male leaders shy away from showing emotions. When appropriate, boys need to see men express and talk about emotions. If we've experienced some sort of hurtful experience, we can let the boys into the emotions of that moment. Perhaps when talking about Jesus weeping over Lazarus, we can tell a story about a time we wept over a loved one. Or we can mention a moment that was so filled with joy that we laughed for five minutes straight. Helping our boys articulate and use their emotions wisely is a key component to raising boys into noble men.

The primary emotion a boy driven by testosterone experiences is anger. Anger is neither good nor bad. It's all in how it is used. Jesus modeled appropriate anger whenever he came face-to-face with injustice—the injustice of an illness, someone being ostracized, or abuse of the temple. His anger moved him to act to fix the injustice, to put to rights what was wrong. Boys need that kind of vision for their anger—to follow Jesus in using anger for good.

Key #5 to Speaking "Boy": Use Competition

Testosterone often expresses itself in competition. Boys love to take each other on. They often come alive when they find themselves battling against other boys for the status of winner, whether that battle is a game of basketball, a trivia contest, a game of cards, or bragging rights over whose NFL team or dad is the best.

Have you ever noticed how boys and men always try to outdo each other in storytelling? Tom tells his friends about how he and his dad went on a five-mile hike on Saturday. Jose has to one-up him by talking about the time he and his dad ran a 10K together. Duon chimes in with the biggest of them all: He and his dad did a four-day hike in Yosemite and slept under the stars. Duon wins! Boys are constantly competing in life.

Sometimes before starting a session with boys, I'll take them out for some friendly competition. It might be a free-throw shoot-out or a thumb-war battle or a football toss. I always give the winners a small prize (usually a piece of candy). I want to teach the boys that in life we win and lose, but good men learn to win and lose with grace.

At other times, I'll connect a teaching with a competition. For example, I'll break the boys into two teams. Each team gets a basketball. When I say go, a boy from each team tries to score a basket. The first one to make the basket gets a point for his team. His team then gets to answer a review question. If the team gets it right, they get two more points. This gets the boys moving, taps into their innate hunger for competition, and moves the learning into their souls.

Key #6 for Speaking "Boy": Call Boys into a Masculine Spirituality

Just as congregations tend to speak, teach, and worship to the way girls/women are wired, they also tend to talk about spirituality in more female-oriented language as well. For example, the primary language used in talking about the God-human connection is "having a personal relationship with Jesus." Boys and men rarely use relational language like that. They talk about hanging out. Or pal-ing around. Or doing stuff together. Bill never says to Chavez, "I want to have a personal relationship with you!" Bill might say, "Do you want to hang out?" Or "Do you want to do something?" Men and boys don't have personal relationships with other men and boys. That's girly language. And Jesus never used that language. He used action language. "Follow me!"

For many congregations, healthy spirituality is expressed through regular Bible reading. But reading tends to favor girls and discourage boys. That's not to say that Bible reading isn't important. I first read through the entire Bible in seventh grade and have done so many, many times since. I think it's crucial that followers of Jesus immerse themselves in the primary stories about Jesus. I regularly encourage boys to read through Mark because the story is fast and active. But if the marker of discipleship for boys is reading the Bible, most will feel like failures.

What boys need is an action-driven masculinity. One that smells of Old Spice, not Chanel No. 5. That action-driven masculinity starts with following Jesus. Masculine faith pledges its sword of power to Jesus and his Kingship, joining him in his bold, daring, reckless adventure of saving the world. A compelling spirituality for boys calls boys to *do* what Jesus did: feed the hungry, heal the sick, fight against injustice, lead with courage, stand against evil, put to rights what is wrong in the world, and love one's neighbor as one's self, all in the context of love and sacrifice. Masculine spirituality calls boys to follow Jesus into every area of their lives from their thought life to their family life to their school life to their friendship life to their work life. Masculine spirituality calls boys, not into community, but into a band of brothers (and sisters) devoted to the cause of Jesus.

When following Jesus is the starting point for male spirituality, when pledging our allegiance to him is the essence of that spirituality, it follows that boys will want to learn all they can about Jesus (through worship, Bible reading, study, etc.) and what it means to follow him into heroic manhood.

Boys understand this kind of following. Look, for example, at how boys follow their favorite sports team. They know each of the players, what the players do, and what their strengths and weaknesses are. They know the season schedule. They know the injury reports and the stats and the over/under. They wear the team colors and live or die by how the team does. They talk about the game with their friends. They watch the game with their friends. They read about their team. They cheer on their team. They learn as much as they can about their team. Their entire lives revolve around their sports team. Boys know how to follow!

> *Boys want clear rules and directions. They also want relevance—a clear line drawn from their lessons to their lives. They want to be protected from public shaming ... and they want to be recognized—sometimes by a quiet gesture, sometimes with great fanfare in front of their peers—when they succeed. To be successful in school* (author's note: or in discipleship) *boys want connection: mentors, guides, and most of all, caring teachers ... Lessons must be taught with passion.[4]*

An Important Interlude

You can't talk about boys, manhood, and faith without talking about sex. As boys start experiencing daily multiple bursts of testosterone, sex and sexual thoughts will consume them. At times, they will experience seemingly uncontrollable sexual energy coursing through their bodies. Everywhere they look, they will see provocative sexual and sexualized images of girls and women, further stimulating that sexual energy. The TV shows, video games, and movies they consume strongly suggest that sexual conquest makes a boy into a man.

Few boys have anyone who will talk openly and honestly with them about sex, their thought life, and their bodies. The sex talk from Mom and/or Dad may last a few moments. (In the PBS special *Raising Cain,* a teenage boy told host Michael Thompson that the sex talk with his dad consisted of Dad saying, "You know you need to use a condom!") The sex talks in school focus more on biology than on a healthy, Jesus-shaped, noble view of sex. Where do most boys get their sex education? From their friends—and they make it up as they go.

Boys need brave men (and women!) to step up and talk openly and honestly about sexual thoughts, masturbation, pornography, treating girls with respect, the gift and sanctity of sex, and the setting of boundaries and sticking to them. What might it look like in your congregation to equip parents to talk with their boys about sex (and we need to be talking about it in appropriate ways starting in about third grade if not earlier)? What might it look like to surround boys with good (not perfect) men to walk with them for a few years as they come to terms with their growing sexual awareness and energy? What does it look like for a boy to follow Jesus in this area of his life? The call to bring even his sexuality under the kingship of Jesus is one a boy needs to hear often in order to prepare him for the onslaught of inappropriate sexual expressions he will encounter as he moves into high school and college.

(*A word for our female readers:* Whereas, generally speaking, women are stimulated sexually first and foremost by touch and conversation, boys and men are stimulated sexually first and foremost by sight, as they are visual creatures. For the next forty-eight hours, I invite you to wear "boy glasses" and see the world the way our boys do. Look at the way girls and women dress. Look at the images of women in TV ads and TV shows. Look at magazine covers. Look at the women in video games. Take forty-eight hours and experience the nonstop bombardment of sexual images pelting our boys 24/7. It will help you understand why forging a healthy spirit of sexuality in our boys is so vital to their impending manhood.)

Two Final—Vital—Keys for Speaking "Boy"

Key #7: Love the Boys

Boys crave male attention. Boys long for connections with men they respect. Boys thirst for the respect, admiration, affirmation, and blessing of other men. Boys need men to love them. Far too many boys have no father figure in their lives—no man who will validate them or pour male energy into them. No amount of high-energy worship, competition, action, or metaphors can do for a boy what a man's investment in a boy can do. What better place to experience dynamic, healthy, transforming love than the church—through men committed to following Jesus by pouring themselves into boys.

A mobile home park sits about one mile from our campus. In many ways, it is an island of at-risk kids in a suburb. The elementary school where we used to worship encouraged us to invest ourselves in the kids in that park. One of the things we did was offer a running program for the boys and the girls. One mom told us that her son was so excited to go to the next session that he waited by the door of his house for five hours, ready to burst out and join the group. She said, "These boys have no men in their lives! They crave men."

Boys also need the love women give. Women tend to love differently from men, and boys need a healthy dose of both.

Key #8: Point Them to Jesus

This ought to permeate everything we do with boys. But I put it here to remind us of the unique gift the church has to offer boys. The church not only can forge in boys a vision for manhood, we can also point them to the One who can lead them into that vision, empower them for that vision, and transform them into good, honorable men.

Jesus offers a boy everything he needs to be a man. Jesus himself is a captivating presence. How can a boy not be attracted to a guy who battles demons, fights against injustice, heals and feeds people, and has such a strong sense of who he is? Jesus, as we've seen, is a man who is in touch with his emotions in a healthy way. Jesus is action-oriented. He gets things done. He's tough enough to take on the enemies of justice and gentle enough to hold children in his arms. He's brave enough to give his life to save the world. When all is said and done, Jesus has the back of each boy. Jesus accepts and stands by each boy, no matter what. That can inspire greatness in boys.

Jesus is the compelling vision for manhood, and the call to follow him is exactly what a boy is looking for. The question is, can he hear that call in our congregations?

7

Building a Boy Friendly Church

> "We had to celebrate and rejoice, because this brother of yours was dead and has come to life; he was lost and has been found" (Luke 15:32).

Research suggests that Tom Sawyer has a 70 to 90 percent chance of leaving the church—leaving your congregation—and not coming back. Those odds favor no one—Tom, his family, the Christian church, or the community in which Tom will live as a man. We can reverse that trend, however, in part by implementing the ideas presented in this book.

Reversing that trend, however, requires not only implementing boy-accessible discipleship principles, but also reorienting the culture of the local congregation around reaching boys. Without a passion for reaching boys and their families embedded into the DNA of the congregation, implementing effective strategies for discipling boys will end up about as effective as the latest diet—lots of enthusiasm to begin, but a loss of will when it proves to be tougher than expected.

Speaking from experience, reaching boys is an immense amount of fun. Seeing boys light up when a Bible story connects, when they receive an affirmation from a Christian man, when they make a stand for Jesus, or when they show glimpses of honor and goodness provides reasons to rejoice. But reaching boys takes some good, hard work and commitment. A congregation committed to being boy friendly is a congregation committed to doing what it takes to find the Tom Sawyers in their community and bring them to life through the call of Jesus. To steal from the old proverb, it takes a congregation to call and empower a boy to follow Jesus into manhood.

A Call to Pastors

Below you will find some practical ideas for creating a boy friendly culture in your congregation. But first, a crucial starting point. Creating a boy friendly congregation begins with the pastor. My bias: Pastors are called to lead. Good leaders keep their ears tuned to God *and* the congregation. Good leaders, through prayer, wisdom, and their own spiritual intuition, lead their congregations where God wants them to go. More often than not, the pastor is somewhat— sometimes a lot—out in front of his/her people. That's as it should be. God calls leaders to lead. The depth of a boy friendly vision in a congregation will reflect the leadership and commitment of the pastor. A boy friendly culture can only be inculcated through the leadership of the pastor.

So, pastors, I'm calling you out! I'm challenging you to learn all that you can about boys; to do all that you can to create a passion in your congregation for finding the Tom Sawyers in your church and community and inviting them and their families to follow Jesus. Join me in starting a revolution to change the storyline of our boys. The following ideas will guide you and your lay leaders in this process. Surrounding yourself with some like-minded leaders will go a long way in embedding this new vision into your church.

(To state the obvious, this is a book about boys. When talking about boys to my congregation, I try to give equal time to a vision for reaching girls as well. However, because the church faces a boy crisis, extra attention needs to be placed on boys until the vision has captured the imagination of the congregation. You can expect some pushback from a few who feel you are talking too much about boys. But keep at it. While intuitively many know a boy crisis exists in the culture and in the church, most can't articulate the problem or know what to do about it.)

Build a Boy Awareness into Your Congregation

While many people have a sense that our boys are in crisis, most people and most congregations have little to no actual awareness of the current storyline of boys. After sitting through my workshops and seminars, moms, dads, grandparents, and church leaders constantly tell me that they understand for the first time why their sons, grandsons, or the boys in their congregations act the way they do.

More than that, very few people in our congregations realize how deeply the boy crisis affects the future of our congregations, a crisis in which so many boys and men are leaving the church. Very few church members realize what a mission field our boys are. In many ways, we still live with a 1960–1970 mind-set that our girls are behind the boys … that our girls need advocacy over and against our boys. Hopefully, this book has convinced you that our boys need us to step up and help them rewrite their story.

Congregations build an awareness of many different issues and groups in our communities from the homeless to the working poor to the unchurched to those living in other countries. But rarely if ever do we paint a picture of the life of boys in our culture today.

I do at least one sermon a year on boys in our congregation (and on girls too) to give people insights into the potential and challenges that make up our sons and grandsons. When I do a parenting message, I often include something about boys. From time to time, I'll recommend a book about boys (see Appendix B). We have even purchased five or six copies of a book on boys and lent them out (and we usually don't get them back!). I have held "summits" on boys, presenting much of the material in this book to groups of men, women, and educators in our church. Because we celebrate the boy's rite of passage several times a year at Grace, I have the opportunity to not only talk about boys, but also to introduce our congregation to the boys in our church.

Building awareness of the storyline of boys in the twenty-first century is crucial for creating a vision for captivating boys and their families.

Embed a Bold, Compelling Boy Vision into the DNA of Your Congregation

While building awareness, you will want to harness the energy of that awareness and turn it into a big, bold, vision for captivating boys. That vision needs to be big enough to motivate passion in your people and practical enough to engage them in tangible ways.

Our congregations' vision is to call and equip boys to follow Jesus into heroic manhood—to partner with parents, grandparents, and educators in transforming the current storyline of boys. We implement that vision in a variety of ways (many of them already mentioned): mentoring boys in our Grace Adventure Club, offering a rite of passage program for junior high boys, inviting boys sixteen and over to join their dads in our Call to Compelling Manhood experience, creating environments where dads can publicly affirm their sons, supporting educators in learning about how boys learn (more below), and calling and equipping men to mentor boys.

What is the vision your congregation has for boys? In what ways will you carry out that vision?

Train Men to be Men (and Mentors)

If the men in our churches have no vision for manhood, they can't lead boys into manhood. Calling and training men to follow Jesus into compelling manhood not only benefits boys, it creates stronger families, stronger congregations, and stronger communities.

Training is the key word here. Many churches have men's ministries but very little strategic training takes place in leading men into manhood. Most men's ministries study a topic, a book, or a book of the Bible but take little time to intentionally connect it to a man's vision for manhood.

Just as a rite of passage program asks boys, "What kind of a man do you want to be?," a strategic men's program at some point needs to ask men the same question and then lead them into a vision that connects their manhood to Jesus.

At least once a year, I preach a message geared to men (and usually more than once). Father's Day provides an obvious opportunity to talk to men and dads about following Jesus into manhood. A message on Adam, how he lost his manhood and how Jesus restores it; or on Jacob and his "male" path to faith; or on Samson and his out-of-control male pursuits; and other sermons on men in the Bible give plenty of illustrations for men.

Robert Lewis developed a fantastic twenty-four-week adventure called *The Quest for Authentic Manhood* (see Appendix B). While it's lecture-based, I've used it twice, and the men find it extremely practical and engaging. *Authentic Manhood* covers everything from the wounds men grow up with to a vision for manhood to how to be a good dad and husband. You can either watch Robert's presentations or you can teach the sessions yourself (which I chose to do).

Every five to six weeks, we hold what we call the *Man-Cave All-You-Can-Eat BBQ*. For ten dollars, the men can eat all they want. After we eat, we do some kind of interactive competition (from thumb-wars to volleyball to basketball competitions). Then I lead the men in a strategic discipleship move. A few examples:

- I already mentioned the *Man-Cave* in which the men brought their sons (and the following month their daughters) and publically affirmed their boys in front of the rest of the men. More than talking about the need for the blessing, we provided men the opportunity to actually do it.

- One year, we held a *Man-Cave BBQ* one week prior to Valentine's Day. For weeks, I hyped it by saying that after this particular *Man-Cave*, the men would go back to their wives, and the wives would respond with a big, huge kiss—guaranteed. But I didn't tell the men what we were going to do for fear they wouldn't come. After we ate, I had one of our staff women come in and lead the men through the process of making a handmade Valentine. At first, the men groaned, but then the competitive testosterone kicked in as they tried to outdo each other in creating their Valentine. We put some Barry Manilow music on in the background to set the mood, and off they went. We took a picture of all the men and their

Valentines and sent the men home. The following week, one of the wives came up to me and kissed me on the cheek for getting her husband to make her a Valentine!

• For one *Man-Cave,* I had the men bring their spouses/ significant others. After dinner, my wife led the women as they filled out a question/answer sheet about their lives. I took the men and had them fill out that same sheet, answering the questions based on how their wives would answer them. Then I instructed the men to go back into the room, grab their wives by the hand, and take them out for a walk. While on the walk, the men were to say three things to their wives. "I love you. This is what I love about you. Before we die, this is what I would love to do with you." What an amazing sight watching forty guys walking around the campus with their spouses, talking together. Afterward, a man in his seventies told me he said things to his wife he hadn't said in years! A few moments later, his wife came up to me. Not knowing her husband had just talked to me, she told me we needed to do this more often, as her husband said things to her she'd never heard before.

Again, the point of a *Man-Cave BBQ* is to get the men together to actually do a discipleship move.

One of the by-products of training men to be men, as it relates to the focus of this book, is that we are training men to be mentors. While we've covered this topic already, one more story will summarize the power of mentors for boys.

Years ago, *60 Minutes* ran a story about a group of juvenile delinquents who were harassing and killing white rhinos, an endangered species. The game wardens knew it wasn't poachers doing the killing because the rhino horns weren't removed. Soon they discovered the killers were male teenage elephants.

Years earlier, another reserve in South Africa had been overrun by the elephant population. The game wardens decided the only way to handle it was to kill off the adult elephants and move the young elephants to a new reserve. The unintended consequence:

The boy elephants had no bull elephants to keep them in place, to put boundaries around their growing testosterone-charged power. Without strong role models and bull elephants to establish hierarchy and teach the young males how to act, the teenage elephants grew increasingly violent.

At first, the wardens tried to solve the problem by killing off the rebel elephants. Then they found a better, more effective, humane solution. They brought some male bull elephants into the reserve. Instantly, the culture changed. The bull elephants put the teens in their place, created a safe hierarchy, and gave the young elephants a "vision" for what it means to be a good elephant.

Our boys need bull elephants in their lives. In training men to be men, congregations provide a way to train men to be good, noble, bull elephants.

Train Dads to be Dads

Many dads have no idea how to raise their sons (or their daughters), as many dads didn't have a dad who provided a good role model for fatherhood. Most dads make it up as they go along, with no real vision or strategy for pouring themselves into their sons. Many of the ideas for Training Men to be Men can be used to train dads to be dads. A couple of resources:

- *Following Jesus: A Heroic Quest for Boys*, as I wrote earlier, not only calls boys into manhood, but also provides a strategic way for dads to invest in their sons. (See Appendix B.)

- *Raising a Modern Day Knight*. Robert Lewis created this experience for dads. In a six-week course, dads learn some strategic father-moves and then go home and implement what they learned with their sons. *Modern-Day Knight* gives dads a pathway for intentionally raising their sons into honorable men. (See Appendix B.)

Offer Opportunities to Equip Parents to Raise their Sons

Parenting classes, books on boys, sermons on parenting, small groups for parents, and a host of other opportunities enables the church to partner with parents in raising their sons.

Support Moms of Boys

I remember when our son Mike entered puberty. Like many boys at that age, he began to withdraw, especially from Mom. One day, Jan asked me why her son hated her. Many moms go through that same thing. Providing moms with knowledge about boys and why they distance themselves from Mom, what it means, and how to deal with it will give moms (and their sons) the tools they need to navigate those important but difficult waters. Support groups for moms with boys and training moms to be moms of boys can give moms the courage they need to pour themselves into their sons.

Don't Forget Your Educators

One of our congregations' missions is to support our public, private, and charter school educators by providing free continuing education opportunities for them. Working with the school districts, we bring in people like Michael Gurian and Michael Thompson to lead sessions for educators, the community, and our members. The educators receive credit for attending, and we have the opportunity to introduce them to speakers they may not get to hear due to the limited budgets schools now work with. We try to schedule these events on a Saturday so we can use the speakers at worship on the weekend.

It may not be feasible for your congregation to fund an event like that on your own, but perhaps along with some other local congregations you can pull it off.

What might it look like for your congregation to roll up its collective sleeves and create a congregation committed to doing whatever it takes to raise up a new generation of boys who follow Jesus into manhood?

Afterword:
Does the Church Really Care about Boys?

I received an e-mail from a man in Australia who had seen our rite of passage program for boys. He said that the Australian church like the US church is losing boys at a rapidly increasing rate. And then he added, "Most churches don't really care or want to know, it seems."

On the one hand, I know what he's talking about. There are pastors (most of them male) who cry, "Stereotyping!" and "Patriarchal thinking!" at the suggestion that we need to do something to stop the hemorrhaging of boys from our churches before they even take the time to look at the issue. Upon being introduced to our boy's rite of passage program, people immediately respond with the question, "Do you have something similar for girls?" Book publishers say (with regret) that there is no market for books on boys geared to church leaders. Apathy exists among leaders and parents to engage with the issue on any level. Secular culture has seen an explosion of books on the subject of boys and how they are falling behind in every area of life (see Appendix B). Secular culture sees what the church doesn't seem to see.

On the other hand, I see energized people rolling up their sleeves and starting the search for the Tom Sawyers in their communities once they hear the current storyline of boys. I see men rising up to take the lead in mentoring boys. I see moms and educators light up with understanding when someone articulates in the concrete what they are experiencing with their sons and male students. I see youth leaders and pastors investing in rites of passage programs to strategically train boys to be men. It's a slow quiet revolution, but one that can change the world.

Does the Church care about boys? Does your church care about boys? Is there a sense of urgency over the fact that we are losing this generation of boys? Have we thought through the implications of generations of men-less churches?

I'm one person who cares deeply about our boys. I know there are others of you out there who also care. Jesus used a small band of men and women to change the world. Will you be among that small band of men and women who will change the storyline of our boys?

If you won't do it, who will?

Appendix A:
Can't Girls be Heroes Too?

I've received pushback from time to time on the connection between boys and heroes and my emphasis on calling boys into heroic manhood. The pushback goes something like this:

Why does boy equal hero? Girls can be heroes too!

This kind of thinking is patriarchal.

You are stereotyping!

In Christ, there is neither male nor female.

I absolutely agree that girls and women can be and are heroes. But that's not the point when it comes to reaching boys. Hero language is boy language. Heroism—saving the world—is an overarching boy/man theme, which we see again and again throughout history and literature. Heroism calls to a boy differently than it does a girl. It's not that girls aren't heroes. It's that boys resonate deeply with that call and language. Heroism is embedded in their DNA. Testosterone—the primary male hormone—is the energy of superheroes.

Saving Private Ryan is a prime example of that compelling theme for boys and men. As Private Ryan stands at the gravesite of Captain John Miller, he remembers back to how Captain Miller and his band of soldiers saved him. With his dying breath, Captain Miller says to him, "James, earn this. Earn it!" James Ryan, now an old man, turns to his wife and asks, "Have I been a good man?"

Do you hear the heart call of every boy and man? Heroism. Being a good man. Saving the world. These are themes woven into the DNA of boys and men by their Creator. Girls can be and are heroes. But boys live their lives based on that theme.

A further challenge to hero language goes like this:

> Jesus was the anti-hero. He lived a life of submission, not heroism.

> Using hero language may pander to boys and men, but it is not biblical, Christ-centered language.

I would argue differently. I recognize that Jesus was not the Messiah the Jews expected—a conquering hero-king-warrior who would overthrow the Roman Empire and establish a new kingdom. He was, indeed, the Messiah who chose servanthood and death in order to save the world. Many people in my opinion misinterpret the kind of Savior Jesus came to be. They paint a picture of passivity. A picture of giving up. A picture that in their minds expresses everything that is antithetical to the hero.

I would suggest that Jesus is the ultimate hero, not the anti-hero; that Jesus defines heroism. Jesus was in control of every moment of his life. He chose to lay down his life. He intentionally served. This was no weak man standing passively before Pilate, Herod, the soldiers, or even hanging on the cross. This was a man fully in tune with his call to save the world—a man who demonstrated true heroism by the deliberate giving of his life. A man who shows that true heroes serve others sacrificially.

As Jesus battled demons and sickness, he was saying, "This is what a hero does." When he washed the feet of his disciples, he was saying, "This is what a hero looks like." When he rode into Jerusalem on a donkey, claiming to be Caesar in a country occupied by the Roman Empire—a provocative act of treason—he was saying, "This is what a hero does." As he hung on the cross, begging his Father to forgive those who nailed him there, Jesus was saying, "This is what a hero looks like." Jesus poured new meaning into heroism, fulfilling the deepest yearnings of the image of God-male. Boys and men aspire to that noble, sacrificial manhood. Jesus not only models it; he empowers boys and men to live it.

The plethora of superhero movies over the last few decades reflects the yearning of culture for heroes and the yearning of boys and men to be heroes. Yes, girls like superhero movies too. But why do you think the producers of these films are so concerned that their movies be well received by boy fans? Because they know that heroism is the heart language of boys.

If you want to reach boys, call them into heroic manhood. It's the language they speak. It's the call they hear. It's the call of their Creator to follow the true hero—Jesus—and save the world.

Appendix B:
Sample Lessons

At our church, children in kindergarten on up start in the worship service with their parents. During communion (which is in the first part of our service), families commune together, and then the parents take their kids to the Grace Adventure Club, and the parents return for the rest of the service (the offering, the sermon, and the blessing). Research tells us that children who attend Sunday school but not "big people worship" are less likely to attend worship as adults than are children who attend worship but not Sunday school. We offer the best of both worlds: worship with the big people and Sunday school during the sermon time. Our Sunday school (the Grace Adventure Club) lasts about thirty minutes.

Below are a few sample lessons I wrote for our coaches (Sunday school teachers) and the boys (third through sixth grade). We call the boys Sunday school class a "huddle." Each session includes an activity that ties in with the lesson. In the first three samples, each boy paints a shield and each week adds a picture on the shield representing a biblical virtue or character quality. I had one of our men make the shields for the boys. I also offer a couple of lessons built around a sword, again put together by one of our men. Sometimes a theme overlaps these sample lessons, but they were presented over a period of a few years. I chose them because they offered some variety in ideas.

You will notice that the lessons don't seem to go very deep. The strategy is this: bond with the boys. Provide activities that help "image-strate" the main point of the lesson. Keep the main point of the lesson focused and memorable. This isn't about pouring information into the boys. It's about forming the boys through mentoring, games, a teaching, and an object lesson. We want boys to be able to articulate what they learned in a sentence or two.

The Power of the Shield

#1—The Purpose of a Shield

Theme: God is our shield—he is our protection

Object: The shield the boys will be making

Begin: Go around the huddle (group of boys) and ask the boys what they are thankful for. (Write down their names so you can pray for them during the week. You may want to get their email addresses if they have them—or the e-mail address of their parents—to write them a quick note during the week about what you talked about during the huddle and to remind them that you are praying for them.)

Lead the boys in the Lord's Prayer.

Take the boys out for a quick free-throw-shooting contest.

Huddle Lesson:

Can anyone tell me what the purpose of a shield is? *(To protect, etc.)*

Back in ancient and medieval times, the shield was used to protect a soldier or warrior from arrows, swords, or clubs during a battle or attacks.

Today, we don't use a lot of arrows, swords, or clubs in war, and yet we still use various forms of shields, not only in battle, but also in everyday life. In fact, there are all kinds of different shields people use today. You may even use them without realizing that they are shields.

Hand out sticky notes and a pen. Ask the boys to write down on each sticky note answers to this question (one answer per sheet): What kinds of shields do we use in our modern world? What kinds of things do we wear to shield or protect ourselves? *Tell them they have ninety seconds to write down as many answers as they can think of.*

If the boys seem stuck, suggest one of these to get them going. You can tease out the other ones if needed. *Windshields on cars … sun glasses (shields our eyes from the sun) … sunscreen (shields our skin from sunburn) … tanks … bulletproof vests … force fields in science fiction … clothes. Have the boys read off one of their answers and put the sticky note on the wall.*

Does anyone know what shape a police badge is? It's the form of a shield because the police serve as shields for the community. Their job is to protect us.

The Bible often refers to God as our shield. Here's what Psalm 18:1–2 says (*perhaps ask if one of the boys wants to read it*), "I love you, O LORD, my strength. The LORD is my rock, my fortress, and my deliverer, my God, my rock in whom I take refuge, my shield … my stronghold."

The writer of that psalm describes the protective nature of God using several different images to describe how God is a shield of protection:

God is his rock. What do you think he means by saying that God is a rock? *(God is strong and cannot be broken.)*

God is his fortress. What do you think he means by saying that God is his fortress? *(God is like a strong castle that the enemy cannot get into.)*

God is his deliverer. God is the one who will save him from hurt.

God is his shield. God is the one who will protect him from the arrows and swords of life that will try to hurt him.

Have the boys jot down a few answers to this: What are some of the things in life that we need God to protect us from? *(Worry, sin, guilt, hurt feelings, etc.)*

As we make these shields the next few weeks, they will remind us that God is our shield. He is the one who will protect us.

Paint an overcoat on the shields. As you do so, engage the boys in bonding conversations about school, sports, etc.

End: *Ask the boys if there is anyone that they want you to pray for who might need God's protection.*

Parents Handout *(hand to the parents or to the boys to take to their parents)*

Parents,

Today the boys began working on making a shield. We talked about what shields do—how they protect us. We also looked at Psalm 18:1–2 where the psalmist talks about how God protects us, calling God his shield.

Here are a few ideas to talk about throughout the week that will help cement the promise of God's protection in your son's heart:

*Talk about the different things around your house that protect the family. You might walk around the house—inside and outside—to discover the various ways the house protects the family.

*Talk about things that make you afraid at times, where you feel you need protection.

*Talk about how God protects us.

Each night, as everyone is getting ready for bed, take a few minutes with your son to do the following:

- Talk about one thing that didn't go so well for each of you today. Offer one thing you are thankful for from the day.

- Read Psalm 18:1–2. Reading it through each night for a week will help you begin to internalize it.

- Pray together. Thank Jesus for the day. Ask him for a good night's sleep. Ask him for a good day tomorrow.

The Power of the Shield

#2—Protection

Theme: God is our shield

Object: The shield the boys will be making

Begin: Go around the huddle and ask the boys what they are thankful for. (Write down their names so you can pray for them during the week. You may want to get their e-mail addresses if they have them—or their parents' e-mail address—to write them a quick note during the week about what you talked about during the huddle and to remind them that you are praying for them.)

Lead the boys in the Lord's Prayer.

Play a brief game with the boys (try a thumb war—last man standing wins a prize).

Huddle Lesson:

Review: Can anyone tell me what the purpose of a shield is? (*To protect*)

Back in ancient and medieval times, the shield was used to protect a soldier or warrior from arrows, swords, or clubs during battle or attacks.

Last week, we talked about how God is our shield, how God's love and forgiveness protects us.

We looked at Psalm 18:1–2 which says, "I love you, O LORD, my strength. The LORD is my rock, my fortress, and my deliverer, my God, my rock in whom I take refuge, my shield ... my stronghold."

We saw that God protects us, and he does so using his strength and power.

The apostle Paul invites us to put on the armor and the protection of God.

> Finally, be strong in the Lord and in the strength of his power. Put on the whole armor of God, so that you may be able to stand against the wiles (temptations) of the devil ... take the shield of faith, with which you will be able to quench (stop) the flaming arrows of the evil one. (Ephesians 6:10–11, 16)

Because God is strong, we can be strong. As we follow Jesus, he is our shield of faith that protects us. He protects us from the arrows of the Devil.

Give the boys a pad of sticky notes. Have them jot down answers to this question (one answer per page): What kinds of arrows does the Devil shoot at us? *(You may need to give the boys a jump-start answer like negative thoughts ... out of control anger ... hatred, unhappiness, guilt, temptation, greed, pride, essentially anything that robs us of life or joy, anything that leads us away from God's best.)*

This morning, we're going to continue working on our shields, and as we do, I hope you'll remember that God is your shield—he is the one who protects you.

*Work on the shields. If the shields need another coat of paint, have at it. Using paint, create four quadrants on the shield. In the top left quadrant have the boys paint a cross. Have them write **faith** under the cross. As you do so, engage the boys in bonding conversations about school, sports, etc.*

End: *Ask the boys what they would like to pray about. Pray that Jesus would be their shield throughout the week.*

Parents:

The boys continued working on their shields. Today, we reviewed the lesson from last week on how God is our shield. This week, we talked about how Jesus is the shield who protects us from the flaming arrows of the Devil. You might ask your son what some of those arrows might be.

Each night, as everyone is getting ready for bed, take a few minutes with your son to do the following:

- Talk about one thing that didn't go so well today. Share one thing you are thankful for from the day.

- Read Ephesians 6:10–11, 16. You might talk about what each of you thinks the armor of God is and what the shield of faith is. Reading it through each night for a week will help you begin to internalize it.

- Pray together. Thank Jesus for the day. Ask him for a good night's sleep. Ask him for a good day tomorrow.

The Power of the Shield

#3—Generosity

Theme: God calls us to arm ourselves with generosity.

Object: The shield the boys will be making

Begin: Go around the huddle and ask the boys what they are thankful for. (Write down their names so you can pray for them during the week. You may want to get their e-mail addresses if they have them—or their parents' e-mail address—to write them a quick note during the week about what you talked about during the huddle and to remind them that you are praying for them.)

Lead the boys in the Lord's Prayer.

Play a quick game of bumpout basketball.

Huddle Lesson:

Review: Can anyone tell me what the purpose of a shield is? (*To protect*)

A couple of weeks ago, we talked about how God is our shield, how God's love and forgiveness protects us. Today, we're going to look at one of the ways in which God shields us.

Ask the boys to think about the best gift they ever gave to someone else. You may want to tell a story first from your own life to give the boys some time to think up something. You may need to prompt them with: What did you give your mom for Christmas? Your dad for Father's Day?, etc.

Does anyone know what John 3:16 says? (*"For God so loved the world that he gave his only Son …"*)

The Bible tells us that God is a generous God. That he loves to give his children gifts, the best gift being Jesus.

Activity: *Divide the boys into two teams. Each team will have an adult. Give each boy some sticky notes and a pen. When you say start, have them write as many different things they can think of, one word per paper, that God gives to us. Give them about forty-five seconds. Stick the answers on the wall, discarding any duplicates. The team with the most answers wins.*

God gives us all kinds of good things because he loves us. He gives us life, hope, forgiveness, family, food, each new day, etc. His best gift, as we said before, is Jesus, who generously gave the gift of his own life so that we could be forgiven.

As his followers, he wants us to be generous people as well. To use our talents to help others. To share our things with others. And to support others and God's work through the giving of some of our money. Being generous shields us or protects us from being greedy and unhappy.

Activity: *Have the boys paint a present in the bottom left corner of their shield and write generosity under it. As you do so, engage the boys in bonding conversations about school, sports, etc.*

End: *Ask the boys what they would like to pray about. Pray that Jesus would fill them with thankfulness for what they have and a willingness to be generous.*

Parents:

Today the boys continued working on their shields, focusing on generosity—being a giving person like Jesus. Here are a few ideas to talk about throughout the week that will help them put into action the concept of generosity.

*Remind your son of a special gift he gave you on Christmas, your birthday, Father's Day or Mother's day, and how much it meant to you.

*Talk about times when you've seen your son being generous to others with his time, talents, stuff, and money.

*Talk about how generosity works in your life and your commitment to giving.

*Talk about one specific way you as a family can be more generous.

*Each night, as everyone is getting ready for bed, take a few minutes with your son to do the following:

- Talk about one thing that didn't go so well for each of you today. Share one thing you are thankful for from the day.

- Read John 3:16 throughout the week to remind each other of God's generous heart.

- Pray together. Thank Jesus for the day. Ask him for a good night's sleep. Ask him for a good day tomorrow.

The Power of the Sword

#1

Theme: God calls us to use our growing power as boys for good.

Object: The sword (Before this lesson, you will want to have one of your men make swords out of wood that the boys can paint over the next few weeks.)

Begin: Go around the huddle and ask the boys what they are thankful for. (Write down their names so you can pray for them during the week. You may want to get their e-mail addresses if they have them—or their parents' e-mail address—to write them a quick note during the week about what you talked about during the huddle and to remind them that you are praying for them.)

Lead the boys in the Lord's Prayer.

Head outside for a quick game of football.

I want to tell you a story—a story that some of you have heard before.

A long time ago, Uther Pendragon *(Pendragon means head dragon, or chief warrior, or king)* was king of Britain. When he died, various men tried to take over as the king of Britain.

But Uther had a son. Does anyone know the name of this son? *(Arthur)*

No one knew of Arthur because Merlin the Magician took the boy, at the request of Uther, when Arthur was a baby in order to protect him. Even Arthur didn't know he was the king's son.

When the time came for Britain to choose its new king, a church service was held, and the people prayed that God would give them a sign of how they should find their new king. Does anyone know what that sign was? *(A sword embedded in white marble.)*

The stone read, "Whoever pulls this sword out of the anvil is the rightful heir and king of Britain."

Knight after knight, prince after prince tried to pull the sword out. But no one was able to get it out of the stone.

Years later, most had forgotten about the sword. Then one day, Arthur's brother (though he wasn't really Arthur's brother) was to ride in a contest. But he needed a sword. Arthur remembered seeing the sword in the stone. Not knowing about the legend, Arthur ran over and pulled it out of the stone. By doing so, he demonstrated that he was the king of Britain.

The sword is a symbol of power. It's a symbol of the gifts and talents God has given to each of us. Noble boys/men use their power—their gifts and talents—for good, they use their sword to help others. To serve others. To protect others.

Ephesians 2:10 says it this way, "For we are God's workmanship, created in Christ Jesus for good works" (author's paraphrase).

Hand out the swords and have the boys begin painting them with an overcoat.

Go around the room as the boys work on their swords and ask each of them one thing they are good at. Affirm their answer as an illustration of the sword or power God has given them to serve him. You will want to take some time on this, especially with a boy who doesn't think he's good at anything to tease out of him something he really likes to do—which may indicate his "power" or talent.

Jesus invites you to use your growing power as a boy to serve him. To follow Jesus as your king. To pledge your sword to him. And he will help you use your power for good, to help others, to make the world a better place.

Ending: *Pray that God will empower the boys to use their powers, their gifts, in honorable, good ways.*

Parent handout

What am I good at?

Mom/Dad,

We are making swords in the Grace Adventure Club and learning that the sword is a symbol for a boy's growing power—for the gifts and talents God has given to him. We used Ephesians 2:10 as our Bible verse. You may want to look it up and have your son read it to you.

Spend some time this week with your son and ask him what he thinks he's good at. Point out to him what you see as his areas of strength and give some examples of and stories about how you see those gifts in action.

You might even talk about some of the things you think you're good at—what gifts and talents God has given you—and how you use them in your life.

We'll continue to talk about this the next few weeks, looking at what it means for the boys to pledge their swords to Jesus—to follow him so that he can use their gifts and talents for good and noble purposes.

The Power of the Sword

#2—The Sword in Action

Theme: God calls us to use our growing power as boys for good.

Object: The sword the boys will be making

Begin: Go around the huddle and ask the boys what they are thankful for (try to get them to focus on something good that happened this past week!). (Write down their names so you can pray for them during the week. You may want to get their e-mail addresses if they have them—or their parents' e-mail address—to write them a quick note during the week about what you talked about during the huddle and to remind them that you are praying for them.)

Lead the boys in the Lord's Prayer.

Go out and play! Or find and indoor game like rock-paper-scissors.

Activity—talk:

Today the boys can name their swords (in literature, the great swords were given names by their owners—something that represented the sword owner or a name for the sword that suggested what it would be used for—Arthur and Excalibur, for example). Have them decorate their sword with symbols and paint the name on it. As they work, engage the boys in the following talk and questions:

While you guys continue working on your swords, I want to talk with you a bit about how Jesus wants us to use our swords.

Can anyone tell me what the sword symbolizes? *(Our power, or the gifts and talents God has given to us.)*

Each of us has been given special gifts and talents by God. And as we follow Jesus, he leads us to use those gifts and talents to help others.

115

Let me tell you a story. It's actually a story Jesus told about a man who used his sword of power for good.

Once upon a time, a Jewish man was walking from Jerusalem to Jericho. It's a walk of about fifteen miles or so. Back in Jesus' day, it was a dangerous walk in that bandits would hide in the rocks and rob the travelers. That's what happened to this man. Robbers stopped him, beat him up, took his money, and left him to die on the side of the road.

A Jewish priest walked by and saw the Jewish man bloodied and dying on the roadside. But he crossed the street and walked on by without helping him. A Levite, a man whose job it was to help run the Jewish temple, also walked by the dying man. And when he saw him, he, too, crossed the street and passed him by without helping him.

Then a Samaritan came walking down the road. The Samaritans and the Jews were bitter enemies. They hated each other.

Can you think of groups of people who hate each other? For example, Cardinals fans hate Cowboys fans. *(You may need to tease out a few other examples with the boys to get them thinking—certain cliques in their school, maybe gangs that hate each other, racial groups, etc.)*

Even though the Samaritans and Jews were enemies, the Samaritan stopped to help the dying man. He bound up his wounds, carried him to a hospital, and offered to pay the entire bill.

Unlike the two Jewish men who walked on by, the Samaritan used his power—his sword—to help a person in need, even though that person was his enemy.

What are some ways in which we can serve Jesus by using our swords to help others? *(Help out around the house. Help a friend who's in trouble. Help out a neighbor …)*

Does anyone have a story about how you helped someone who was in trouble? *(Leader—tell a personal story if you have one to get the boys thinking.)*

When Jesus says we are to love our neighbors as we love ourselves, he's inviting us to use our swords to help others just as Jesus used his sword to help us by dying for us and rising again so he could forgive us.

Ending/Prayer: *Go around the room to see what the boys might like you to pray about.*

Using the sword for good

Mom/Dad,

We are making swords in the Grace Adventure Club and learning that the sword is a symbol for a boy's growing power—for the gifts and talents God has given to him.

This week we focused on the story of the Good Samaritan. You might want to read it together: Luke 10:25–37.

Tell your son a story about a time you saw him using his sword for good—helping out someone. Have him tell a story about a time he helped someone that maybe you don't know about.

Christmas

#1—The Gift of Christmas

Theme: God gave his best gift

Object: The boys will be making a manger out of clay.

Begin: Lead the boys in the Lord's Prayer.

Play a quick game outside.

Huddle Lesson:

Have the boys write down on their sticky notes why we give gifts—the reason for gift giving. Give them sixty seconds. Have the boys stick the notes on the wall and talk through why we give gifts.

At Christmastime, God gave us his best gift—the gift of Jesus. The Bible says that "God so loved the world"—he loves each one of us so much—"that he gave his only Son Jesus, so that everyone who believes in him may not perish but may have eternal life" (John 3:16). God gave us his best gift ever. His son, Jesus, who died for us and rose again so we could be forgiven.

Can anyone tell me what he wrapped that gift in? *("They wrapped him in a blanket, and laid him in a manger" (Luke 2:12)).*

God didn't use fancy wrapping paper with Rudolph or Santa or Christmas trees on it. He wrapped Jesus in a blanket, and put him in a feedbox—a box out of which animals ate their dinner!

Today, we're going to make a manger. But I want you to see a picture of a real manger. Normally, the mangers we see at Christmas are made of wood. But mangers in Jesus' day were really made out of stone or clay. Imagine how hard and cold that must have been for

Jesus being a new baby. That's why his mom wrapped him in a blanket and probably laid him on a pile of hay.

(Find a manger picture on the Internet)

Have the boys mold a manger out of the clay. They can make it as creative as they want to. Perhaps you might say, "Create a manger that you think you would want to put the baby Jesus in if he were born today."

Chat with the boys during this time about school, about Christmas coming up, what they want for Christmas, etc.

Ending: *Have the boys share one thing they are thankful for as your closing prayer.*

Parents:

Today the boys began looking at the story of Christmas. We focused this week on giving the best gift ever and how Jesus was God's best gift to us. We also looked at why we give—and how God gave Jesus because of his love for us.

We talked about how we wrap Christmas gifts, and we saw that Jesus was wrapped in a blanket and placed in a manger.

Ask your boy why his manger is made of clay.

Sometime this week, talk together about the best gifts you've ever given to others and why it is that we give gifts.

Each night, as everyone is getting ready for bed, take a few minutes with your son to do the following:

- Talk about one thing you are thankful for from the day.

- Read John 3:16 and remind yourselves of the great love God has for us, shown in the great gift of Jesus.

- Pray together. Thank Jesus for the day. Ask him for a good night's sleep. Ask him for a good day tomorrow.

Christmas

#2—The Promise of Christmas

Theme: God's promise is that Christmas is for all of us.

Object: The boys will be making shepherds and sheep out of clay.

Begin: Ask the boys what they are thankful for and lead them in the Lord's Prayer.

Christmas Quiz Competition:

Break the boys into two teams (or, if there are not enough boys for teams, have the boys compete against each other.) If in teams, each boy is given a balloon. Have one boy from each team step up front. With their balloons filled with air, they will be asked a question. The first boy to "squeak" in by squeezing out some air from his balloon gets first crack at the question. Each correct answer is worth two points. If he gives the wrong answer, the other team gets a chance to steal the answer for one point. The team with the most points wins and gets a piece of candy. (Have one of the men keep score.)

If not enough for the teams, each boy gets to "squeak" in for each question using his balloon. If the first to squeak in gets it right—two points. If he gets it wrong, ask the question again, and the next boy to squeak in first gets to steal the question for one point. The winner gets a piece of candy.

Questions:

- Where does Santa usually land his sleigh? *(On the roof)*

- In what village was Jesus born? *(Bethlehem)*

- What was Jesus' dad's name? *(Joseph—or God!)*

- What color is the Grinch? *(Green)*

- What famous Christmas-hater was Bob Cratchit's boss? *(Scrooge)*

- To whom was the birth of Jesus first announced? *(Shepherds)*

- What are Frosty the Snowman's eyes made out of? *(Coal)*

- Who first announced the birth of Jesus? *(Angels)*

- Who is the Red-nosed Reindeer? *(Rudolph)*

- What is the first name of the real Santa Claus? *(Nicholas)*

- Bonus Question-worth ten points: On what day of the year do we celebrate the birth of Jesus? *(December 25)*

Huddle Lesson:

Ask the boys to think for a moment about the students who go to their school. Ask them to describe the various cliques that they observe—the kids who hang together and don't allow others into their groups. Give them sticky notes and have them write down as many cliques as they can think of (you may have to jump-start their thinking by suggesting a clique or two—the jocks, the video-game fans, etc.).

Put the various cliques on the wall. Look at a few and ask a question, such as, "What kinds of students are not allowed into the jock clique? The cheerleader clique? The video-game fanatics clique?"

In life, people oftentimes surround themselves with friends, and this circle of friends won't let others into their group. Cardinals fans, for example, may not allow Seahawks fans into their group. Or jocks won't allow band geeks into their group. Or white people won't allow black people into their group. There are insiders—those who are accepted into a group, and there are outsiders—those who aren't allowed into a group.

In Jesus' day, there were groups like that as well. The rich didn't allow the poor into their circle of friends. The religious didn't allow the nonreligious into their group. Women weren't allowed into areas set aside for men.

One group of people almost no one included in their circle of friends was shepherds. In Jesus' day, shepherds were looked down upon as dirty liars. They smelled because they were always with sheep. They were dirty because they lived out in the fields with the sheep. And for whatever reason, they couldn't be counted on to tell the truth. In fact, they had such a bad reputation that a shepherd could not be a witness in a court case. No one would believe him. No one wanted to hang out with shepherds. They were the outsiders.

But when Jesus was born—the Savior of the world—the news wasn't first announced to the in-crowd—to the rich or the religious. It was announced to the outsiders—to the shepherds—to the people no one wanted to include in their circle of friends. But by announcing the birth of Jesus to these hated, smelly, shepherds, God was saying that he loves everyone, and that everyone is invited into his circle of friendship through Jesus.

To remind us that God's love includes us, that Jesus invites us, too, to follow him, we're going to make some shepherds and sheep to include in our manger scene we began making last week. *(If some of the boys did not make a manger, have them make one along with their shepherds and sheep.)*

As you and the boys make the shepherds, talk with them about how school is going, what their Christmas plans are, tell them yours, talk about your job, etc. This is the time to bond with the boys.

The boys can take their shepherds/sheep home with them to add to their manger scene.

Ending: *Ask the boys what they'd like you to pray about. End with prayer*

Parents:

This week, we looked at how the birth of Jesus was first announced to the shepherds. This was actually quite remarkable in that shepherds were despised by almost everyone. They were dirty and smelly and known as liars. They were the outsiders. And yet God chose to announce the birth of Jesus to these outsiders first, reminding us that Jesus is for all of us—that we are all invited into God's circle of friends.

You might ask your boy about where he feels he fits in at school. Who are his friends? Perhaps ask him who don't include him or who his friends won't include? You may tell stories from your own life when you felt included, excluded, or when perhaps you excluded others. Remind each other that God's love in Jesus includes us too!

Have him put his latest addition to his expanding nativity set—shepherds and sheep—in a place where it will remind you all of the story of Christmas.

Each night, as everyone is getting ready for bed, take a few minutes with your son to do the following:

- Talk about one thing you are thankful for from the day.

- Read Luke 2:8–10 and remind yourselves that Jesus is for all people, including us.

- Pray together. Thank Jesus for the day. Ask him for a good night's sleep. Ask him for a good day tomorrow.

Christmas

#3—The Good News of Christmas

Theme: The Good News of Christmas: A baby—a Savior—has been born for us.

Object: The boys will be making angels out of clay.

Begin: Ask the boys what they are thankful for and lead them in the Lord's Prayer.

Play some kind of quick, competitive game and give the winners a candy reward.

Huddle Lesson:

Give each boy a section of a newspaper. Have them look for one story they consider to be good news. Give them about three to four minutes. Have each boy give a quick report on what story he chose and why he considers it good news.

When Jesus was born, the angels announced the birth with these words, "Do not be afraid; for see—I am bringing you good news of great joy for all the people; to you is born this day in the city of David a Savior, who is the Messiah, the Lord" (Luke 2:10).

What do you think makes the birth of Jesus good news? What's so good about it? What does Jesus give us that makes his birth good news? *(Give the boys a chance to come up with some answers.)*

This morning we're going to finish up our manger scenes by making angels. The angels remind us that the birth of Jesus is good news of great joy, and that we too are called to tell others about this good news. But before we make them, what are some ways in which we can tell others about the good news of Jesus?

While the boys work on their angels, use the time to talk with them about school, their plans during Christmas vacation, what gifts they might be buying for family, etc.

The boys can take the angels home.

Ending: *Pray with the boys, asking God to fill them with Christmas joy so that they will share the good news of Jesus with their friends.*

Parents:

This week, we focused on the news the angels shared—the good news of great joy. Ask your boy what he thinks makes the birth of Jesus good news. Tell him what you think makes it good news. Talk about some ways in which you as a family can be like the angels and tell others about the good news of Jesus.

Have your son put his latest addition—the angels—to his expanding nativity set. Place the nativity where it will remind all of you of the story of Christmas.

Each night, as everyone is getting ready for bed, take a few minutes with your son to do the following:

- Talk about one thing you are thankful for from the day.

- Read Luke 2:8–14 and remind yourselves that Jesus is the good news of great joy!

- Pray together. Thank Jesus for the day. Ask him for a good night's sleep. Ask him for a good day tomorrow.

Appendix C:
Resources

Programs:

Following Jesus: A Heroic Quest for Boys. Tim Wright and Michael Gurian. www.heroicquestforboys.com

Raising a Modern Day Knight. Robert Lewis. www.rmdk.com

The Quest for Authentic Manhood. Created by Robert Lewis. www.mensfraternity.com

Knights of the 21ˢᵗ Century. Created by Roy Smith. www.KnightsOfThe21stCentury.com

Fathering Adventures (Australia). A weeklong experience that equips and empowers dads to guide their sons into authentic manhood. www.fatheringadventures.com.au

The Gurian Institute offers a wide variety of programs for educators using brain science research. www.GurianInstitute.com

Books:

Janet Sasson Edgette and *Beth Margolis Rupp:*

The Last Boys Picked: Helping Boys Who Don't Play Sports Survive Bullies and Boyhood. New York: Berkley, 2012.

Michael Gurian:

The Wonder of Boys: What Parents, Mentors and Educators Can Do to Shape Boys into Exceptional Men. New York: Tarcher/Penguin, 2006.

The Mind of Boys: Saving our Sons from Falling Behind in School and in Life (with Kathy Stevens). San Francisco: Jossey-Bass, 2005.

The Purpose of Boys: Helping Our Sons Find Meaning, Significance, and Direction in their Lives. San Francisco: Jossey-Bass, 2009. (This book served as the template for *Following Jesus: A Heroic Quest for Boys*.)

Boys and Girls Learn Differently: A Guide for Teachers and Parents (with Kathy Stevens). San Francisco: Jossey-Bass, revised edition, 2010.

A Fine Young Man: What Parents, Mentors, and Educators Can Do to Shape Adolescent Boys into Exceptional Men. New York: Tarcher/Putnam, 1998.

The Good Son: Shaping the Moral Development of Our Boys and Young Men. New York: Tarcher/Putnam, 1999.

Nurture the Nature: Understanding and Supporting Your Child's Unique Core Personality. San Francisco: Jossey-Bass, 2007.

How Do I Help Him? A Practitioner's Guide to Working with Boys and Men in Therapeutic Settings. Spokane: Gurian Institute Press, 2011.

Mitchell P. Davis and Roy Smith

Bull. Pennsylvania Counseling Services, Inc., 2012. bull@knightsofthe21stcentury.com

Michael Kimmel

Guyland: The Perilous World Where Boys Become Men (Understanding the Critical Years Between 16 and 26). New York: Harper, 2008.

Robert Lewis

Raising A Modern-Day Knight: A Father's Role in Guiding His Son to Authentic Manhood. Carol Stream: Tyndale House, 2007.

Donald Miller

Father Fiction: Chapters for a Fatherless Generation. New York: Howard Books, 2010.

David Murrow

Why Men Hate Going to Church. Nashville: Thomas Nelson, 2005, 2010.

Michael Reichert and Richard Hawley

Reaching Boys, Teaching Boys: Strategies that Work and Why. San Francisco: Jossey-Bass, 2010.

Leonard Sax

Boys Adrift: The Five Factors Driving the Growing Epidemic of Unmotivated Boys and Underachieving Young Men. New York: Basic Books, 2007.

John Sowers

Fatherless Generation: Redeeming the Story. Grand Rapids: Zondervan, 2010.

Michael Thompson

Raising Cain: Protecting the Emotional Life of Boys (co-authored with Dan Kindlon, with Teresa Barker). New York: Ballantine Books, 1999.

It's a Boy: Understanding Your Boy's Development from Birth to Age 18 (with Teresa Barker). New York: Ballantine Books, 2008.

Peggy Tyre

The Trouble with Boys: A Surprising Report Card on Our Sons, Their Problems at School, and What Parents and Educators Must Do. New York: Three Rivers Press, 2008.

Richard Whitmire

Why Boys Fail: Saving Our Sons from an Educational System That's Leaving Them Behind. New York: Amacom, 2010.

Debby Zambo and William G. Brozo

Bright Beginnings for Boys: Engaging Young Boys in Active Literacy. Newark: International Reading Association, 2009.

Tedd Zeff

The Strong, Sensitive Boy: Help Your Son Become a Happy, Confident Man. San Ramon: Prana Publishing, 2010.

Video:

Raising Cain: Exploring the Inner Lives of America's Boys (featuring Michael Thompson). PBS Home Video, 2006.

Notes

[1] Michael Kimmel, *Guyland: The Perilous World Where Boys Become Men* (New York: Harper, 2008), 269.

Part 1—Searching for Tom Sawyer: Boys in the Twenty-first Century

1. Tom Sawyer: Lost in the Twenty-first Century: A Story about Boys

The information for this chapter comes from a large variety of sources but two books are prominent: *Why Boys Fail: Saving our Sons from an Educational System that's Leaving them Behind*, Richard Whitmire (New York: Amacom, 2010), and *The Trouble with Boys: A Surprising Report Card on Our Sons, Their Problems at School, and What Parents and Educators Must Do*, Peg Tyre (New York: Three Rivers Press, 2008).

[1] Mark Twain, *The Adventures of Tom Sawyer*, chapter 1, http://www.literaturepage.com/read/tomsawyer-2.html

[2] Michael Thompson and Teresa Barker, *It's a Boy: Your Son's Development from Birth to Age 18.* (New York: Ballantine Books, 2009); xiv.

[3] Twain, chapter 6, http://www.literaturepage.com/read/tomsawyer-38.html

[4] Michael Gurian, *The Purpose of Boys: Helping Our Sons Find Meaning, Significance, and Direction in Their Lives* (San Francisco: Jossey-Bass, 2009), 16.

[5] Michael Reichert and Richard Hawley, *Reaching Boys, Teaching Boys: Strategies that Work and Why* (San Francisco: Jossey-Bass, 2010), ix.

[6] Twain, chapter 5, http://www.literaturepage.com/read/tomsawyer-34.html

2. Why Do Boys Do That?

[1] Dan Kindlon and Michael Thompson, *Raising Cain: Protecting the Emotional Life of Boys* (New York: Ballantine, 1999, 2000), 32.

[2] Michael Gurian, *The Wonder of Boys* (New York: Tarcher/Penguin, 1996, 2006), 6–15.

Part 2—Forging the Spirit of Boys: Changing the Storyline of Boys

3. A Motivating Affirmation for Life

[1] Full quote from a lawyer in Turkey: "In our villages, everyone works very hard together to craft our boys into men. We become afraid of them if we don't. The last thing we want is for men to carry empty souls in their big bodies." Gurian, *The Purpose of Boys*, 8.

[2] Kimmel, 130.

4. A Compelling Vision for Life

[1] Twain, chapter 8, http://www.literaturepage.com/read/tomsawyer-61.html

[2] Howard Pyle, *The Story of King Arthur and His Knights*. (New York: Sterling, 2005), p. 100.

[3] Janet Sasson Edgette and Beth Margolis Rupp, *The Last Boys Picked: Helping Boys Who Don't Play Sports Survive Bullies and Boyhood*. (New York: Berkley Books, 2012), 181.

[4] Pyle, 143–144.

5. An Empowering Strategy for Life

[1] Kimmel, 42.

[2] Ibid., 100.

[3] Ibid., 83.

[4] A typical description of a Lutheran confirmation process:

Confirmation is the process for youth to learn and experience the Christian faith in preparation for affirming the baptismal vows made by their parents.

In Christian love, you have presented these children for Holy Baptism. You should, therefore, faithfully bring them to the services of God's house and teach them the Lord's Prayer, the Creed, and the Ten Commandments. As they grow in years, you should place in their hands the Holy Scriptures and provide for their instruction in the Christian faith, that, living in the covenant of their Baptism and in communion with the Church, they may lead godly lives until the day of Jesus Christ. – *Lutheran Book of Worship*

And so, becoming adult members of the Christian community, we ask youth to affirm these vows for themselves, having spent time in study and fellowship and service to understand and experience those things which we are asking them to confirm.

You have made public profession of your faith. Do you intend to continue in the covenant God made with you in Holy Baptism:

To live among God's faithful people ... To hear his Word and share in his Supper ... To proclaim the good news of God in Christ through word and deed ... To serve all people, following the example of our Lord Jesus ... And to strive for justice and peace in all the earth?

In order to inspire and instruct our youth to be adult leaders in the church who will fulfill these vows, we have our confirmation program, involving the following elements:

Class instruction in...

- how to read and understand the Bible

- the Old and New Testaments

- Martin Luther's Small Catechism

- Lutheran Doctrine and History

- prayer and Spiritual Growth

Part 3—Forging the Spirit of Your Congregation: A Church for Boys

6. Speaking "Boy"

[1] Twain, chapter 4, http://www.literaturepage.com/read/tomsawyer-26.html

[2] Ibid., 29.

[3] Reichert and Hawley, 65.

[4] Ibid., x

About the Author

Tim Wright has been an ordained pastor in the Evangelical Lutheran Church in America since 1984. His first call took him to Community Church of Joy in Glendale, Arizona, a Lutheran mega-church. Tim served as the associate pastor on staff for almost twenty-two years. In addition to managing the staff, he oversaw the worship of Joy and launched and managed Joy's leadership center for over fifteen years. Under Tim's direction, Joy's leadership center hosted yearly conferences for pastors and church leaders, featuring the most innovative Church leaders of the day. In addition, he offered seminars on worship, preaching, and leadership across the United States and in Germany, Finland, Norway, France, England, New Zealand, and Australia. During that time, he authored five books: *A Community of Joy: How to Create Contemporary Worship; Effective Evangelism: More Than Getting Them in the Door; The Contemporary Worship Handbook; The Ministry Marathon: Caring for Yourself While Caring for the People of God;* and *The Prodigal Hugging Church: A Scandalous Approach to Mission in the 21st Century*.

In 2005, Tim planted a new congregation out of Joy called Community of Grace in Peoria, Arizona. Early on in that church start, he began to recognize the loss of boys and men in church and felt called to do something about it. As a result, he started *Tim Wright Ministries*, creating resources for churches to call men, boys, women, and girls to follow Jesus, using Community of Grace as a laboratory for the programs and concepts.

Tim lives in Glendale, Arizona, with his wife, Jan. They met in high school and have been married since 1979. They have two children and three grandchildren (so far), all of whom live within miles of their home. Tim enjoys reading British mysteries, watching British mysteries, and riding his bike out on the canals of Phoenix. He's convinced heaven will look a lot like Disneyland at Christmas.

Tim can be reached at tim@timwrightministries.org

About Tim Wright Ministries

Tim Wright Ministries partners with parents, church leaders, and educators in changing the current storyline of boys and girls. The role of TWM in this partnership is the creation of practical tools and resources designed to equip congregations to call boys and girls to follow Jesus into honorable manhood and womanhood. These tools utilize a grace-based theological perspective combined with the latest in brain science research. Resources include a rite of passage for junior high boys, *Following Jesus: A Heroic Quest for Boys,* and a complimentary experience for junior high girls, *Following Jesus: A Journey of Wisdom for Girls.* Other resources available are seminars, consultation, and DVDs.

For more information about these resources, booking a seminar with Tim, or for further inquiries, go to www.timwrightministries.org. Also, "like" us at www.facebook.com/HeroicQuestsforBoys.

LEAD YOUR BOYS INTO HEROIC MANHOOD WITH THIS ONE OF A KIND RITE OF PASSAGE EXPERIENCE
FOLLOWING JESUS: A HEROIC QUEST FOR BOYS

Created by Pastor Tim Wright *(Searching for Tom Sawyer)* and Michael Gurian *(The Wonder of Boys)* this Boy's Quest Kit provides everything your congregation or dads/sons small group needs to empower boys to hear the call to follow Jesus into Heroic Manhood.
TO ORDER: www.heroicquestforboys.com
For more information contact Jeff@heroicquestforboys.com

Made in the USA
San Bernardino, CA
18 February 2016